THE ART OF LOVE

AND OTHER LOVE BOOKS OF

OVID

Ovid's ART OF LOVE *has been called, in the words of the* Encyclopaedia Britannica, *"perhaps the most immoral book ever written by a man of genius." Its erotic brilliance appealed to the prevailing taste of the fashionable world of Ovid's day, an era of gross moral laxity, and has continued to fascinate readers for nearly 2000 years.*

Written in the elegant and graceful language of sophisticated Augustan Rome, the first two books of the ART OF LOVE *contain advice for the predatory male. The third book is devoted to aiding the female in her pursuit of the male. All three books are cast in the conventional form of the erotic Alexandrian elegy, but are graced with Ovid's unique wit.*

This volume also contains Ovid's other love books: THE LOVES, *in which he wrote about his mistress Corinna;* LOVE'S CURE, *a prescription for falling out of love; and* THE ART OF BEAUTY, *some further advice to the fair sex.*

It is interesting to note that of all the ancient poets, it was Ovid who made the most powerful impression on such writers as Marlowe, Spenser, Shakespeare, Milton and Dryden.　　　UL-61

THE ART OF LOVE

AND OTHER LOVE BOOKS

OF

OVID

(Publius Ovidius Naso)

ILLUSTRATED BY
FEDERICO CASTELLON

The Universal Library
GROSSET & DUNLAP
NEW YORK

PRINTED IN THE UNITED STATES OF AMERICA

CONTENTS

BOOK I—THE LOVES

THE ART OF LOVE

THE LOVES

BOOK I

EPIGRAM

We who of late numbered five books, are now but three. 'Twas Ovid our author willed it so. If you win no joy from reading us, the abstraction of two books will at least lessen your displeasure.

ELEGY I

THE POET EXPLAINS HOW IT IS HE COMES TO SING OF
LOVE INSTEAD OF BATTLES

I WAS about to sing, in heroic strain, of arms and fierce
combats. 'Twas a subject suited to my verse, whose lines
were all of equal measure. But Cupid, so 'tis said, began to
laugh, and stole away one foot. Who was it, cruel boy, gave
thee this right to meddle with poetry? We poets belong to
the train of the Muses and follow not in thine. What would
be said if Venus were to seize upon the arms of golden-haired
Minerva, and if golden-haired Minerva were to wave thy
lighted torches in the wind? Who would deem it well that
Ceres should queen it o'er the wood-crowned heights, and
that the tilling of the fields should be the quivered Virgin's
care? Shall Apollo, with his glorious tresses, go armed with
the spear, what time Mars wakes into song the strings of
the Aonian lyre? Too great already are thine empire and
thy power; wherefore then, boy, wouldst thou make wider
yet the frontiers of thy realm? Is all the world thine? Shall
Helicon and the Vale of Tempe call thee master, too? Shall
Apollo himself cease to be lord of his own lyre? Brave was
the line that sounded the opening of my new poem, but lo!
Love comes and stays my soaring flight. No boy have I, nor
long-haired girl, to inspire me in these lighter strains.

Such was the burden of my plaint when, on a sudden,
Cupid lowered his quiver and drew forth therefrom arrows
to pierce my heart. Then, bending his curving bow with a
will upon his knee, he said, "Poet, here is matter for thy
song." Ah, hapless me, Love's arrow did but all too surely

find its mark. On fire am I, and Love, and none but Love, now rules my heart that ne'er was slave till now. Now let six feet my book begin, and let it end in five. Farewell fierce War, farewell thy measure too. Only with the myrtle of the salt sea's marge shalt thou bind thy fair head, my Muse, who needs must tune thy numbers to eleven feet.

ELEGY II

THE TRIUMPH OF LOVE

WHO is it that can tell me why my bed seems so hard and why the bedclothes will not stay upon it? Wherefore has this night—and oh, how long it was!—dragged on, bringing no sleep to my eyes? Why are my weary limbs visited with restlessness and pain? If it were Love that had come to make me suffer, surely I should know it. Or stay, what if he slips in like a thief, what if he comes, without a word of warning, to wound me with his cruel arts? Yes, 'tis he! His slender arrows have pierced my heart, and fell Love holds it like a conquered land. Shall I yield me to him? Or shall I strive against him, and so add fuel to this sudden flame? Well, I will yield; burdens willingly borne do lighter weigh. I know that the flames will leap from the shaken torch and die away in the one you leave alone. The young oxen which rebel against the yoke are more often beaten than those which willingly submit. And if a horse be fiery, harsh is the bit that tames him. When he takes to the fray with a will, he feels the curb less galling. And so it is with Love; for hearts that struggle and rebel against him, he is more implacable and stern than for such as willingly confess his sway.

Ah well, be it so, Cupid; thy prey am I. I am a poor captive kneeling with suppliant hands before my conqueror.

What is the use of fighting? Pardon and peace is what I ask. And little, I trow, would it redound to your glory, armed as you are, to strike down a defenseless man. Crown thy brows with myrtle and thy mother's doves yoke to thy car. Thy step-father will give thee the chariot that befits thee, and upon that chariot, amid the acclamations of the throng, thou shalt stand a conqueror, guiding with skill thy harnessed birds. Captives in thy train, youths and maidens shall follow, and splendid shall be thy triumph. And I, thy latest victim, shall be there with my fresh wound, and with submissive mien I will bear my new-wrought fetters. Prudence shall be led captive with hands bound behind her back, and Modesty, and whatsoever else is an obstacle to Love. All things shall be in awe of thee, and stretching forth their arms towards thee the throng with mighty voice shall thunder "Io Triumphe!" Caresses shall be thy escort, and Illusion and Madness, a troop that ever follows in thy train. With these fighting on thy side, nor men nor gods shall stand against thee; but if their aid be lacking, naked shalt thou be. Proud to behold thy triumph, thy mother will applaud thee from High Olympus and scatter roses on thy unturned face. Thy wings and thy locks shall be adorned with precious stones, and all with gold resplendent shalt thou drive thy golden car. Then too, if I know thee well, thou wilt set countless other hearts on fire, and many a wound shalt deal as thou passest on thy way. Repose, even when thou art fain to rest, cometh not to thine arrows. Thy ardent flame turns water itself to vapor. Such was Bacchus when he triumphed over the land of the Ganges. Thou art drawn along by doves; his car was drawn by tigers. Since, then, I am to have a part in thy godlike triumph, lose not the rights which thy victory gives thee over me. Bethink thee of the victories of thy kinsman Cæsar; he shields the conquered with the very hand that conquers them.

ELEGY III

HE COMMENDS HIMSELF TO HIS MISTRESS BY THE
MERITS OF HIS POETRY, THE PURITY OF HIS MOR-
ALS, AND BY THE VOW OF HIS UNCHANGEABLE
FIDELITY

MY prayer is just: let the fair one who has so lately captivated my heart love me ever, or so act that I shall
love her ever. Nay, but 'tis too much I ask! Only let her
suffer herself to be loved. May Cytherea incline her ear to
all my prayers. Vouchsafe thy favors to a lover who swears
that he will serve thee through the years, who knows how
to love with pure and lasting fidelity. If I have no long line
of famous ancestors to recommend me, if the founder of our
family is but a simple Knight; if innumerable plows be not
required to till my fields; if my father and mother are con-
strained to husband our resources, at least let Apollo and his
choir the Nine, and the discoverer of the vine, plead with
thee in my behalf, and Love who gives me unto thee, and
faith that shall fail not, irreproachable morals, guileless sin-
cerity and modesty that knows how to blush. I am none of
those who love a hundred women at a time; I am no fickle
philanderer. Thou and only thou, believe me, wilt ever be
beloved by me. Whatsoever the tale of years the fates may
spin for me, I will pass them at thy side, and, dying, be
lamented by thee.

Vouchsafe to be the joyful subject of my song, and my
songs shall be worthy their theme. 'Twas poesy that gave
renown to the nymph Io, affrighted at her horns, and to the
fair Leda whom the divine adulterer seduced by taking on
the semblance of a swan, and to Europa who, carried off by
a fictitious bull, traversed the sea, grasping in her virgin

hands the wide horns of her captor. We too shall be sung throughout the world, and ever my name shall be united with thine own.

ELEGY IV

OVID, HIS MISTRESS AND HER HUSBAND ARE ALL BIDDEN TO THE SAME SUPPER. HE GIVES HIS MISTRESS A CODE BY WHICH THEY CAN TESTIFY THEIR LOVE FOR EACH OTHER, BENEATH HER HUSBAND'S VERY EYES

YOUR husband will be at our supper. May that supper be his last. So I shall only be looking on my beloved as any other of the guests might look on her. The right to caress her belongs to another. Voluptuously lying at another's feet, his is the bosom thou wilt warm. And when he will, he may pat and stroke thy neck. Marvel no more that, her bridal banquet over, the fair Hippodamia excites the monstrous race of the Centaurs to the combat. I dwell not, as do they, in the forests, nor, as they, am I half-man, half-horse; yet it would, I trow, be full hard for me to restrain my ardor and my jealousy. Now learn what it will behove thee to do and suffer not the winds, neither Eurus nor the warm-breathing Notus, to whirl away my words.

See to it that thou comest before thy husband. I do not surely foresee what, if thou dost so, may befall; yet be there before him. When he shall have lain him down beside the table, go thou, with mien demure, and lay thee at his side, but forget not, as thou passest, to rub my foot, but, secretly, so that he shall not see. Never take thine eyes off me; take heed of all my movements and note the discourse of my eyes. Secretly receive, and secretly send forth, these signals of our love. Though they utter no word, my eyebrows shall speak to thee; my fingers, aye, and the very wine itself shall have their language. When thou bethinkest thee of the delights we taste together, thou and I, pass thy dainty hand o'er the roses of thy cheeks. If there is aught wherewith thou wouldst secretly reproach me, softly, with thy fingers, touch the tip of thine ear. When the signs I make, or the words I speak, delight thee, then be sure, my starry one, to twist thy ring about thy finger.

Touch the table as the priest toucheth the altar, when thou wouldst call down well-merited evils on thy husband. When he shall pour out wine for thee, bid him quaff it himself; then whisper softly to the slave and bid him bring thee the wine thou dost prefer. The cup which thou givest him back, I will drink therefrom, and the place thy lips have touched, there shall my lips touch also. If, peradventure, he offer thee a dish whereof he hath already tasted, put it from thee. Suffer him not to shower upon thee his unworthy caresses. Lean not thy dainty head upon his uncouth breast; let not his roving fingers touch thy lovely breast; and above all, see that there be no kissing. If thou but give him a single one, I will proclaim myself thy lover; I will say, "These kisses are mine," and I'll clap a heavy hand upon him.

These caresses at least I shall behold with mine eyes, but the fondlings that the table-cover shall conceal from my sight, they are the hidden things that will put my soul to the rack. Put not thy thighs nor thy legs nigh to thy husband, nor touch with thy dainty toes his hard and clumsy foot.

Ah, hapless me; countless are the things of this kind that I dread, for countless are the times I have myself indulged in them. All that I myself have experienced with thee, comes back to-day to torture me. Oftentimes my mistress and I, feeling with our hands beneath our sheltering raiment, have forestalled the sweet moment of delight. Thus thou shalt not do, but so thou mayest free me from the merest shadow of misgiving, lay bare thy shoulders from the mantle that enshrouds them. Cease not to bid thy husband drink; but add no kisses to thy prayers; and so long as he shall be able to swallow, stint not secretly to fill his cup with strong wine. When he is overcome by sleep and liquor, we ourselves will do what the place and the circumstances permit.

When thou risest up to return home, all the company will rise with thee; remember then to place thyself in the midst of the throng. There shalt thou find me, or I thee, and then whatsoever part of me thou canst touch, lay thy hand upon it.

Aye me! These my behests can serve but for an hour or two. The imperious night is at hand that severs me from my mistress. Her husband will have her in keep and hold till the day cometh, and I, weeping sad tears, can but follow her to that cruel door. He will taste her lips, and anon far more than her lips. What thou grantest me in secret, he will demand as his right. But this, at least, give him with reluctance, thus much thou canst do, and as one yielding to superior force. Silent be thy caresses and let Venus be niggard with him. If thou fulfillest my behests, he will taste no delight, and thou at least will feel none in his arms. Howbeit, whatsoever may betide to-night, assure me on the morrow that he hath had no joy of thee.

ELEGY V

HIS DELIGHT AT HAVING OBTAINED CORINNA'S FAVORS

'TWAS summer, and already past the hour of noon. I flung myself on my couch to rest my limbs. My windows were but half open. The light of my chamber was like the light of the woods, or like the glow which follows after sunset; or rather, like the twilight that comes between departing night and dawning day. Such is the light that is befitting for young women of reserve; in its mystery their timid modesty may find concealment.

Behold Corinna cometh, her shift ungirdled, her tresses hanging loose on either side her snowy neck. In such guise did the fair Semiramis offer herself to the caresses of her spouse, and thus did Lais give welcome to her many lovers. I raised her shift, which withal was of so fine a texture that it was but a flimsy obstacle. Howbeit Corinna was not willing to be deprived of her raiment. She strove, but not as one whose will it is to conquer. Soon she gave up the struggle and consented to be conquered.

When, her apparel laid aside, she stood naked before mine eyes, not a blemish was to be seen on her whole body. What shoulders, what arms it was my privilege to behold and to touch. What bliss to press a bosom shaped so perfectly for such caresses. How soft and smooth her skin beneath her lovely breasts, how divine her figure, how firm and plump her thighs. But wherefore should I here tell o'er the number of her charms? Nought did I see that was not perfect, nor was there aught, how thin soe'er, between her lovely body and my own. Need I tell the rest? Wearied, we rested from our toil. May many an afternoon be thus sped by.

ELEGY VI

HE CONJURES THE PORTER TO OPEN THE DOOR OF HIS MISTRESS'S HOUSE

HAPLESS porter, laden with unmerited fetters, push me back this cruel door upon its hinges. 'Tis little enough I ask of thee. No, do but open it a little, just enough for

me to pass in sideways. I have long been a lover and it has
so reduced my body and my limbs that such a thing were
easy. 'Tis Love that tells me how to creep in softly in the
midst of the guards. 'Tis he that guides me and safeguards
my steps.

Time was when I dreaded the night and its empty shadows.
I marveled how any one could fare forth in the darkness.
But Cupid laughed in my face with his gentle mother, and
whispered in my ear, "Thou too shalt grow a mettlesome
fellow." Love's hour has come; I fear not the mazy shadows
of the night, nor weapons uplifted against me. I only fear
the slowness of thy movements; thee alone do I cajole; in
thy hands thou hold'st the weapon that can undo me. See—
and that thou may be the more surely convinced, take down
awhile these cruel bars—see how this door is moistened with
my tears. This is I, thou knowest it well enough, who, seeing
that thwackings were about to rain down on thy naked
shoulders, interceded for thee with thy mistress. How now!
Shall my supplications, which erstwhile proved so powerful
in thy behalf, to-day—oh, shame!—prove powerless in my
own? Come, pay back what thou owest; now mayest thou
show thy gratitude to the top of thy bent. The night is
passing—slide back the bolts. Open the door, and so may
thou be freed for ever from thy long chain and from thy
water-drinking serfdom.

Vain are my prayers, O man implacable; harder than iron
is thy heart. Thou hearest me and yet thy door of oak is
barred against me. That a beleaguered town should need
unyielding gates, 'tis well; but in the heyday of peace, what
fear hast thou of arms? How wouldst thou treat a foe, if
thou repel a lover thus? The night speeds on; slide back
the bolts.

I come not as a warrior attended by henchmen. I should
be alone, were not cruel Love beside me. Him, even if I de-

sired it, I could not send away. 'Twere easier to sunder my soul from my body. Love, a little wine in my head, a chaplet slipping from my perfumed hair, these are the things I bring. Who could be scared at *them?* Who would be daunted by such foes? The night speeds on; slide back the bolts.

Is it thy slowness, is it sleep that is no friend to Love, that makes thee heedless of my prayers and flings them to the winds? Yet, if my memory deceive me not, when, once on a time, I sought to evade thee, I found thee astir in the middle of the night. Peradventure at this moment thine own belovèd is reposing at thy side. If this be so, how preferable is thy lot to mine. If it be so, pass on to me, ye cruel chains! The night speeds on; slide back the bolts.

Do I dream? Did not the door swing upon its hinges? Did it not grunt its signal for me to enter? Alas, I was deceived! 'Twas but an unruly gust of wind that made it creak. Ah, hapless me! How far away that gust doth bear my hopes. If, O Boreas, thou dost bethink thee of the ravished Orithya, come swiftly hither and, with thy blast, beat down this heedless door. All is quiet in the city. Moist with diamond dew, the night speeds on; slide back the bolts.

Open, I say, open, or I, better prepared than thou, with my sword and with the fire I bear within my torch, will break into this disdainful house. Night, Love and Wine counsel no half-hearted measures. Night knoweth not shame. Love and Wine know not fear. Everything, prayers, threats have I essayed, but all in vain, nought could avail to move thee, O man more deaf than the door thou guardest! Thou wast not made to guard a lovely woman's door. Thy office should be to keep the key of a loathsome dungeon. But see, the morning star is risen, and the cock's shrill trumpet calls the laborer to his task. And, flowery wreath, which from my brows sadly I disengage, lie there upon this heartless threshold through the night. When on the morrow my mistress shall descry thee trailing there, tell her the hours that, sick at heart, I wasted at her door. Farewell, porter; in spite of all, I say to thee, farewell. Mayest thou thyself suffer the agony of unrequited love. Muddy-mettled villain, who wouldst not give admittance to a lover, fare thee well. And ye too, ye cruel doors with your pitiless hinges, and threshold more slavish than the churl that guards thee, to all I say farewell.

ELEGY VII

HE CURSES HIMSELF FOR HAVING MALTREATED HIS MISTRESS

LOAD my guilty hands with fetters, if thou be my friend, now that my anger has departed. Rage it was, look you, that made me raise my rash hand against my mistress. O madman that I was! To think it was my hand that made her weep! At that moment I would have struck my father and mother; nay, I would have rained blows upon the gods themselves.

But say. Did not Ajax, armed with his sevenfold shield, slaughter the flocks that he seized in the broad meads? And the ill-fated Orestes who, in his mother, wrought vengeance on his father, did he not take arms against the Dark Sisters? And could I, I of all men, dishevel her rangèd tresses? And did this mar my mistress's beauty? Not so, she only looked the lovelier. In such guise they say the daughter of Schœneus, armed with her bow, pursued the beasts on Mænalus. In such a plight did Ariadne mourn, when she beheld the swift south winds bearing away both the sails and the promises of her perjured Theseus. Thus too, O chaste Minerva, but for the sacred fillets that bound her head, Cassandra had lain upon thy temple's floor.

Who would not have called me a madman? Who would not have called me a barbarian? But never a word said she. Her tongue was paralyzed with fear. Howbeit I read the mute reproach upon her face, and, though she spake not, her tears were my accusers. Oh, why did not my arms fall from my shoulders? It had been better had I lost a limb. 'Tis against myself that my violence hath turned, and my vigor hath been the instrument of my own torture. Wherefore do I need you more, ye ministers of crime and slaughter? Avaunt, ye sacrilegious hands, and with the fetters ye deserve, be laden. Why, had I struck the humblest Roman, I should have had to answer for it. Have I then more right to strike my mistress? The son of Tydeus left a hideous memorial of his wickedness. He was the first to raise his hand against a goddess. I am the second. And withal, his sin was not so black as mine. I struck the woman whom I said I loved; he did but wreak his fury on a foe.

Now, mighty conqueror, go and prepare thy triumph. Set the victor's laurel crown about thy brows and on thy knees give thanks to Jove, and let the vast throng that grace thy chariot shout aloud, "Io triumphe!" And let thy poor victim fare sadly before thee, her hair unbraided, pale from head to foot but for the bruises on her cheeks.

Better it had been to have left upon her lips the imprint of my own, better that her neck should bear the traces of my loving teeth. Then, even though I was as violent as a mountain torrent, even if I was beneath the sway of blind rage, was it not enough to shout at the poor girl, without roaring out a torrent of horrible threats and tearing her dress from neck to girdle? 'Twas there my violence stopped? Nay, so hardened was my heart, that I dragged her along by the hair and in my barbarous rage I left the mark of my nails upon her dainty cheek. There she stood distraught, her face as white as Parian marble. I beheld her deathlike look, and her limbs trembling like the poplar leaf stirred by the sighing wind, like the slender reed which bends beneath the zephyr's breath, like the wave whose surface is ruffled by the warm south wind. Her tears, long restrained, coursed down her face as the water floweth from the melting snows. 'Twas then I 'gan to feel the blackness of my guilt. Those tears of hers, what were they but my blood? Thrice I essayed to fling myself, a suppliant, at her knees. Thrice she thrust away my dreaded hands. "Lay on," I cried, "and spare not. Vengeance will alleviate thy pain. Tear my face with thy nails, spare not mine eyes, no, nor my hair. Let rage lend strength to thy hands, weak though they be; or at least, to obliterate the sad traces of my crime, braid once more the tresses that my hand so cruelly disheveled."

ELEGY VIII

HE CURSES A CERTAIN OLD WOMAN OF THE TOWN WHOM HE OVERHEARS INSTRUCTING HIS MISTRESS IN THE ARTS OF A COURTESAN

THERE exists (give ear, all ye who are fain to know a prostitute), there exists a certain old hag named Dipsas. Her name she deriveth from her calling. Never, in a sober state, does she behold dark Memnon's daughter with her steeds of roseate hue. Learned in magic and in the Æan arts, she hath power to turn the swiftest rivers and make them flow backwards towards their sources. Skilled is she in the virtues of herbs, of linseed twisted on the cabalistic wheel, and of hippomanes. She needeth but to wish, and lo, the heavens grow dark with heavy clouds; to wish again, and lo, the heavens shine in purest splendor. I have seen, wouldst thou believe it, blood drip from the stars. I have seen red blood overspread the face of the moon.

I suspect that she, living though she be, flies through the shadows of the night, and that her hag's body is covered with feathers. That is what I suspect, and such is the report. In her eyes shines a double pupil whence rays of fiery light dart forth. She calleth forth the dead from the graves, our grandsires and great-grandsires. At the sound of her incantations, the solid earth doth open. She delighteth to profane the chastity of the marriage bed, and her poisoned tongue is not lacking in eloquence. Chance, on a day, made me a witness of her lessons. I was able, thanks to our double doors, to hear unseen. Thus, then, she spake:

"Dost know, my fair one, that yesterday thou didst please the eye of one of our young favorites of fortune? He spied thee and his eyes never wandered from thy face. And whom, indeed, wouldst thou fail to attract? Thou yieldest in loveliness to none. But, alas, thy raiment is not worthy of thy beauty. Would thou wert rich as thou art fair. Win thou riches, and I shall no more be poor. The star of Mars in opposition hath been unkindly to thee; but Mars hath departed; and now Venus, the protectress of thy sex, hath taken his place. See how favorable to thee his advent is. A wealthy lover desireth thee and is fain to know what thou dost lack. His face and figure as thine own are fair, and if he fain would buy thy charms, so shouldst thou purchase his."

The girl blushed as she heard this. "Modesty," the crone went on, "becometh a fair cheek, but 'tis useless save when feigned. Real modesty is nearly always harmful. When, with downcast eyes, thou gazest modestly on thy bosom, look at none save in proportion to the price he offereth. Maybe, when Tatius was king, the heavy Sabine dames refused to give themselves to more men than one. Nowadays Mars employs our gallants in foreign wars; but Venus reigns in the

City of her beloved Æneas. Enjoy yourselves, my pretty ones. She is chaste whom none hath courted. Or, if coyness doth not hold her back, she herself maketh the first advances. Come now, efface these frowns that delve their lines upon thy brow; with those wrinkles many a failing will be removed. 'Twas with a bow that Penelope tested the strength of her young lovers; and that bow, the index of their prowess, was of horn. Time hurries on, by us unheeded. It fleets away even as a river whose waters ever flow. Bronze is made bright by rubbing; what availeth fair apparel, if it be not worn. The palace that is tenantless decays beneath the moss that molders it. So beauty, if there be none to enjoy, waxeth swiftly old. Nor do one or two lovers suffice. The more there be, the greater is the pay, and the more readily obtained. Rich is the booty that falls to the hoary wolves who seek their prey from a whole flock. Now tell me, what dost thou get from this poet of thine save his latest verses? A few thousand verses, such is the coin in which thy lover payeth. The god of poesy himself, robed in a mantle gold inwrought, touches the chords of a golden lyre. Let him who hath gold to give thee be greater in thy sight than great Homer himself. Mark my words, it does a man good to give. Scorn not the slave who has bought his freedom. 'Tis no crime to have thy foot marked with chalk, nor shouldst thou suffer thyself to be dazzled with the lordly display of a long line of ancestors. Begone and take thy forefathers with thee, thou needy lover. And how now? Here is another who would fain lie a night with thee, because he is comely. Ah, no indeed! Let him go and beg some money for thee from his own admirer.

"Be not over-exacting whilst thou art spreading thy nets, for fear lest the prey should escape thee; but once he is in thy power, fleece him as thou wilt. Simulated love is often no bad thing. Let him think thou lovest. But see thou love not for nothing. Sometimes withhold thy favors. As for a pretext, why, maybe thy head doth ache, or else the festival of Isis compels thee to abstain; but hold not thyself too long aloof, lest he grow used to the lack of thee, or lest love, by dint of being rebuffed, at length grow cold. Let thy door, closed to the needy, be open to the rich. Let the laments of the rejected reach the ears of the favored lover. If thou woundest thy lover, be wroth with him as if he had hurt thee first. Forestall his upbraidings with thine own; but indulge not over-long thine anger. Anger too far prolonged hath oft engendered hate. Let thine eyes learn the secret of shedding tears at will and moistening thy cheek. If thou wouldst deceive, fear not to forswear thyself. Venus makes the gods deaf to the plaints of the deceived lover. Take into thy service a clever man and maid who may indicate what presents you would welcome. Let them also beg a few things for themselves. If they ask a little of many, each separate ear of corn will soon make up a rick. Let thy sister and thy mother and thy nurse lay thy lover under contribution. There will soon be a goodly heap of booty, when several hands labor at the task. Thou lackest a pretext for soliciting a present? Show him a cake and say it is thy birthday.

"Above all, never let thy lover think that he hath no rival; love, without rivalry, endureth not. Let him see upon thy bed the traces of another possessor of thy charms, and on thy neck the marks of his lascivious embraces; and above all, let him behold the gifts his rival hath bestowed on thee. If he brings nought with him, tell him of the novelties they are showing in the Via Sacra. When thou hast dragged from him a goodly tale of presents, bid him not despoil himself entirely, but ask him for a loan—that thou wilt ne'er repay. Let thy tongue beguile him, to conceal thy scheming; caress him, the more surely to lure him to his doom. Sweet honey hides the subtlest poison. If thou followest my lesson, which long experience has taught me, if thou tossest not my words to the winds, how oft, when I am dead, wilt thou pray the gods to let the earth lie lightly upon me."

Thus she was speaking, when my shadow betrayed me. 'Twas with difficulty I kept myself from tearing her last gray hairs, her eyes that were shedding drunken tears, and her cheeks furrowed all over with wrinkles. "May the gods," I said, "reject thee, and send thee a miserable old age, endless winters and an everlasting thirst."

ELEGY IX

HE COMPARETH LOVE WITH WAR

THY lover is a soldier, and Cupid hath his camp. Aye, believe me, Atticus, every lover is a soldier. The age which suiteth war is also favorable to Venus. A fig for an elderly soldier! A fig for an elderly lover! The age which generals demand in a brave soldier is the age which a fair young woman demands in the possessor of her charms. Soldier and lover have, each, their vigil to keep; both couch upon the hard ground; both have their watch to keep, the one at the door of his mistress, the other at the door of his general. What a weary way the soldier hath to march! And the lover, when his mistress is exiled, will follow her, with a stout heart, to the uttermost limits of the world. He will fare over the loftiest mountains and over rivers swollen with rains; he will cleave his way through the snowdrifts. Is he compelled to cross the seas? He will not plead that the tempests are let loose; nor will he wait till the weather be propitious for setting sail. Who but a soldier or a lover will brave the chill nights and the torrents of mingled snow and rain?

The one is sent forward as a scout towards the enemy; the other keepeth watch upon his rival as upon a foe. The one lays siege to warlike cities, the other to the dwelling of his inexorable mistress. One beats down gates, the other doors.

Oftentimes it hath brought victory to catch the foe asleep, and to slaughter, sword in hand, an unarmed host. Thus did the fierce battalions of Thracian Rhesus fall and you, ye captured steeds, forsook your lord. So, too, a lover oft is able to profit by the husband's slumbers and to turn his arms against the sleeping foe. To elude the vigilance of watchmen and sentinels is ever the perilous task alike of the soldier and the lover.

Mars is uncertain and in Venus there is nothing sure. The conquered rise up again, and those you would deem could never be o'erthrown, fall in their turn. No longer then let love be held a little thing. Love demandeth a resourceful mind. Achilles burns for Briseis torn from his embraces. Trojans, while his grief allows, smite ye the Grecian host. Fresh from Andromache's embraces, Hector went forth to battle. 'Twas his spouse who placed his helmet on his head. When he beheld the daughter of Priam, her tresses floating in the wind, the son of Atreus, the first of all the Grecian chiefs, stood, they say, lost in admiration. Mars himself was caught in the chains which Vulcan had forged. No tale made a greater stir in heaven than this. I myself was slothful and not born for work. My bed and sleep had softened my spirit. But love for a comely young woman set a term to my indolence. She enjoined me to make my first campaign in her service. Since then, thou seest me ever active and always busy with some nocturnal adventure. Thou wouldst not be a sluggard? Well then, love a woman.

ELEGY X

HE ENDEAVORS TO DISSUADE HIS MISTRESS FROM BECOMING A COURTESAN

SUCH as she who, snatched away from the banks of the Eurotas in the Phrygian ships, was for her two husbands the cause of so long a war; such as was Leda when cunning Jupiter, hidden beneath the deceptive disguise of a white-plumed swan, seduced her and made her his paramour; such as Amymone wandering in the parched fields of Argos, her urn upon her head; such wast thou in my eyes. I feared for thee the divers wiles that Love suggested to almighty Jove, I feared for thee the metamorphosis of the Eagle and the Bull. But now I fear no more. I am cured of my malady, no more mine eyes are blinded by thy loveliness. How came this change, thou askest? Why, 'tis that thou settest a price upon thy favors. This is the reason why thou pleasest me no more. So long as thou wast artless and free from guile I loved thee body and soul; but now this blemish on thy soul hath robbed thy body of its charms. Love is a child and Love is naked. The years have not corrupted him and he wears no clothes, that he may be without guile. Wherefore dost thou ask the child of Venus to sell his favors at a price? He wears no robe wherein to put the coin. The hard calling of a soldier suits neither Venus nor her son; how befits it, then, that divinities so unused to war should serve for pay?

A courtesan selleth herself for a given price to the first customer; by yielding her body she gaineth her miserable pay. Yet withal she curseth the tyranny of the greedy whoremaster, and what thou doest for thy pleasure, she doth because she must.

Take, for an example, the beasts devoid of reason. Thou

wilt blush to find the brutes possessed of finer feelings than thyself. The mare asks no gift of the stallion, nor the heifer of the bull; the ram payeth not the ewe on whom he wreaks his passion. Woman alone loves to flaunt the spoils she wrests from man. She alone setteth a price upon her favors; she alone offereth herself for hire. She selleth a pleasure that bringeth delight to both, a pleasure which both have longed for, and she maketh him pay for the bliss he giveth her. When love hath equal charms for both, wherefore should one sell it and the other buy? Wherefore should I lose, and thou win, at a game wherein we both minister to our mutual bliss?

A witness may not sell his testimony for money; nor must a judge take bribes. It is a disgrace for an advocate to sell his services to a pauper or for a tribunal to grow fat on the proceeds of justice. So, too, it is shameful for a woman to augment her patrimony by bartering her charms and by selling her body to the highest bidder. Gratitude we owe for a favor freely given, but none for the sordid hiring of a woman and a bed. Once thou hast received thy pay, thy hire—love and gratitude are at an end.

Ah, dear women, never set a price on the favors ye bestow. Ill-gotten gains will never prosper. Of what value were the bracelets of the Sabines to the young vestal who was crushed beneath the weight of their armor? A son plunged his sword into the loins that bore him; a necklace lured him to his crime.

Not that thou shouldst refrain from asking presents of a rich man. He hath the wherewithal to satisfy thy demands. Pluck the grapes that hang from the loaded vines; gather thy apples in the fruitful orchards of Alcinoüs. And for the poor man, bethink thee of the good he doeth thee, of his zeal and his fidelity. Let every man give what he hath unto his mistress. My wealth consists in celebrating in my verse the women who render themselves worthy of that honor. She who maketh me desire, her my art exalteth. Precious gifts and costly raiment will perish; gems set in gold will one day shattered be, but my verses shall endure for ever. What disgusts and enrages me is not giving, but seeing thee ask for pay. What I refuse thee when thou askest, I will freely give thee when thou askest not.

ELEGY XI

HE ASKS NAPE TO DELIVER A LOVE-LETTER TO HER MISTRESS

O THOU who with such happy art dost bind and range thy mistress's hair, thou whom 'twere unjust to place in the ranks of ordinary servants, Nape, as skillful in contriving nocturnal assignations as in conveying missives to my beloved, thou hast often persuaded the hesitating Corinna to come to my arms; thou whose loyalty hath ofttimes saved me in a crisis, take these tablets and deliver them this very morning to my mistress. May thine ingenuity prove triumphant over every obstacle. Thy breast is not made of adamant or steel; nor dost thou carry simplicity to excess. Thou too, methinks, hath felt boy Cupid's darts. Fight then and defend the flag 'neath which we both do march. If she ask thee how I fare, tell her the hopes of spending a night with her keep me alive. For the rest, my passionate hand hath writ it on this waxen tablet.

Even as I speak, time fleeteth away. Go and choose a moment when she's free and give her these; but see to it that she read them straightway. Note her eyes, her brow while she doth read. Her mute expression will inform thee of my fate. As soon as she hath read my words, ask her to indite a long reply. I hate to see blank spaces on the wax. Let her lines be close together, let her writing fill up the margins, so I may feast my eyes upon her letters. Yet wherefore should she weary herself with writing? Let me read but a single word, *Come,* and swiftly I will deck my tablets with the laurels of victory, hang them as a votive offering in Venus' temple, and inscribe them thus: "Unto Venus doth Ovid consecrate you, faithful ministers of his love, which, but a while ago, were but a fragment of worthless maple."

ELEGY XII

HE CALLS DOWN CURSES ON THE TABLETS WHICH BRING HIM WORD OF HIS MISTRESS'S REFUSAL

MOURN and lament with me! My tablets have come back, with this one sad word upon them scored: *Impossible!* I have some belief in omens. Just now, as she went out, Nape struck her foot against the threshold. Henceforth, when thou art sent anywhere, remember to walk more warily and to pick up thy feet. Away with you, ye ill-omened tablets, away, thou sullen wood, and as for thee, thou wax that bringest her refusal, thou wast sucked from the flower of the towering hemlock; surely thou art the dregs of the vile honey of some Corsican bee. Thou seemest to have been stained with vermilion, and truly thou art of bloody hue. Go and kiss the ground, ye useless things; may the heavy wheel of the first cart that passes crush you into atoms. No, the fellow that hacked you from the tree to shape and fashion had filthy hands. That same tree must have served as a gibbet for some unlucky wretch, and furnished the crosses of death to the executioner; beneath its mournful shade the howlet shrieked, and amid its branches the vulture and the screech-owl laid their eggs. To such

wood as this was I mad enough to confide the secrets of my
heart. Such was the wood I bade carry to my mistress the
tenderest words of love. This wax would more appropriately
have served for some crusty lawyer's writ, or for the diary
wherein a miser might record the payments that wrung his
heart. O lying tablets, little wonder that men call ye double;
faith, 'twas a number of evil augury. What is the worst fate
my wrath can wish you? May time devour you and rot you,
and may the wax which covers you grow damp and foul
with mildew!

ELEGY XIII

HE ENTREATS THE DAWN TO HASTEN NOT
HER COMING

LO, over the Ocean doth she come, from the arms of her
aged husband. Over the waves she cometh, the bright
goddess whose car brings back the day. O beautiful Aurora,
whither dost thou hasten? Stay, O stay thy flight. So,
yearly, may the birds make solemn offering to the shades
of Memnon. This is the time when I love to lie in my sweet
one's sheltering arms; this, if ever, is the moment when 'tis
sweet to press her softly to my side. Now, too, sleep is pleasant and the air cool, and the birds discourse sweet music from
their tender throats. Whither fleetest thou, with a speed to
men and to their mistresses unwelcome? Draw in with thy
shining hand the dewy reins of thy swift coursers.

Ere thou risest, the mariner can clearly see the stars, and
wandereth not at random over the wide seas. When thou
dost appear, the traveler, for all his weariness, must quit his
couch, and the soldier seize his fighting gear. Thou art the
first to behold the husbandman shouldering his mattock; the
first to call the lagging oxen to the yoke. Thou robbest chil-

dren of their sleep and handest them over to the master for
their tender fingers to suffer the blows of his cruel ferule.
Thou bringest the surety to the court, where a single word
may make or mar him. To advocate and to judge thou art
alike unfriendly, for each is forced to rise to take up a case.
'Tis thou who, when a woman would fain taste the sweets
of repose, callest her to spin the wool with unwearying
hands. All this I could endure; but who would bear that
young women should rise thus early in the morning, save the
man that hath no mistress of his own? How often have I
longed that night would not make way for thee, that the
stricken stars would not flee before thee! How often have
I longed for the winds to shatter thy car, or for one of thy
steeds to founder in the hollow of a cloud! Ah, cruel one,
whither dost thou hasten? Since thou had'st a son whose
skin was black, such was the color of his mother's heart.
Would that Tithonus were free to speak his mind about thee,
the heavens I trow would ne'er have known a more lascivious
woman. Thou fleest from thine aged spouse, because old age
hath chilled him, and leavest the old man betimes to mount
thy hateful car. But if in thine arms thou heldst thy favorite, Cephalus, thou wouldst cry, "Go slow, go slow, ye
coursers of the Night!"

And though thy spouse be wasted with old age, wherefore should *my* love pay the penalty? Was it I that led thee
to mate an old man? See how many hours of sleep the Moon
gave to the youth she loved; and her beauty is no whit inferior to thine. The father of the gods himself, that he might
not behold thy face so often, joined two nights in one, so as
to let his passions have full play.

Thus did I upbraid her; be sure she heard me, for she
blushed. Howbeit the day appeared no later than his wont.

ELEGY XIV

TO HIS MISTRESS, WHO, CONTRARY TO HIS COUNSEL,
DYED HER HAIR WITH NOXIOUS COMPOSITIONS,
AND HAS NEARLY BECOME BALD

DID I not say to thee, "Cease to dye thy hair?" And
now thou hast no longer any hair to dye. Nevertheless, hadst thou not been stubborn, where was there anything
more beautiful than thy hair? It came down to thy knees,
so fine thou wast afraid to comb it. No finer is the tissue
with which the dark-skinned Seres clothe themselves; no
finer is the thread which, with her dainty legs, the spider,
swaying from her lonely beam, draws out to weave her airy
web. Howbeit its color was not black as ebony, nor was it
golden. 'Twas a mixture of the two. Such is the color of
the tall cedar in the cool valleys of Mount Ida, when its bark
is stripped away.

So soft, so tractable it was that thou couldst bind it in
countless different ways, without the smallest trouble. Never
did the comb's tooth tear thy tresses; thy tire-woman was
never fearful of a slapping. Many a time have I been present at my mistress's toilet and never did she seize the bodkin
to prick her woman's arms. Sometimes of a morning, her
hair still in disorder, she would lie, half turned over, on the
purple bed. And even then, in her careless abandon, she
was lovely, lovely with the loveliness of an o'er-wearied Bac-
chanal who has cast herself, heedless of her posture, on the
green grass.

Then her tresses were soft as down. How often, alas, have
I seen them put to the torture, compelled patiently to endure
both iron and fire, to make them stay in little rounded curls.
" 'Tis a crime," I cried, "a crime to scorch that hair of thine;

it falls beautifully of its own accord. Cruel one, have mercy
on thine own head. Away with such violent treatment.
This is not the sort of hair to scorch. Thy hair itself in-
structs the bodkin where to go."

Gone are those lovely tresses which Apollo, which Bacchus,
might have envied; such tresses as Dione, coming naked from
the foam, upheld with her dripping hands.

Why, since they pleased thee not, dost thou lament the
ruin of thy tresses? Wherefore, stupid one, dost thou thrust
aside so mournfully thy mirror? No longer doth it please
thee, remembering what thou wast, to gaze therein.

Howbeit 'tis not to magic herbs culled by a jealous rival,
nor to water drawn by some treacherous witch from Hæmonian springs, that their fall is due. 'Tis not the effect
of some dire malady (the gods keep thee from that), no, nor
a rival's jealous tongue, envious of their beauty. No, thine
is the crime, and thine own the hand that wrought the loss
thou mournest; thine own the hand that poured the poison
on thy head. Now Germany will send you some slave-girl's
hair; a vanquished nation shall furnish thy adornments.
Alas, how oft, when thou shalt hear men praise the beauty
of thy hair, wilt thou tell thyself with a brush, " 'Tis purchased merchandise that makes me comely in their sight
to-day; of some unknown Sygambrian girl my friends the
praises sing. Yet I remember the day when that glory was
my own."

Heavens, what have I said? See, she can scarce restrain
her tears. She buries her face in her hands, and look how
she is blushing. She steals a glance at once of her fallen
tresses lying in her lap, a treasure, alas! not fitted for that
place. Nay, come then, soothe thy heart and clear thy brow.
The loss is not irreparable. Ere long with thine own hair,
thou wilt be beauteous as of yore.

ELEGY XV

THE POETS ALONE ARE IMMORTAL

WHEREFORE dost thou blame me, gnawing Envy, for consuming my days in slothfulness; wherefore callest thou my verses the employment of an idle mind? Why dost thou reproach me for not following in the footsteps of my forefathers, for not seeking, while vigorous youth permits, to crown my brows with the dusty laurels of war, for not studying the jargon of the law, or for not prostituting my words in a dingy court of justice? Mortal are the works whereof thou pratest; my aim is glory that shall not perish, so that in every time and in every place I may be celebrated throughout the world. Mæonides shall live so long as Tenedos and Ida shall endure, so long as Simois shall roll his hurrying waters to the sea. The Ascræan bard, too, shall live while the grape ripens on the vine, while the corn shall fall beneath the sickle's curving blade. The song of Battus shall be sung throughout the world, albeit his art, rather than his genius, is his title deed to fame. The tragic buskin of Sophocles shall never grow old. So long as the sun and the moon shall shine, Aratus will live on. So long as slaves are rogues, as fathers storm, as pimps deceive and strumpets wheedle, Menander will not die. Ennius, for all his artlessness, and Accius, with his lusty speech, possess a name that Time shall not lay low. When shall there dawn an age that shall know not Varro, or the first ship to sail the seas, or the Golden Fleece brought home by Æson's son? When the world perisheth, then, and not till then, shall the works of the high-souled Lucretius perish too. Tityrus and the garnered crops, Æneas and his doughty deeds, will be read so long as Rome shall wield her scepter o'er the conquered world. So long as Cupid wields his fires and bends his bow, thy numbers, skilled Tibullus, will remembered be. In the West and in the East the name of Gallus shall be known to fame, and because of Gallus, the name of Lycoris shall live on. What though devouring time wear down the flint, and blunt the share of the enduring plow, yet poetry shall never die. Let kings, then, and all their train of conquests, yield to poetry, to poetry let the happy shores of the golden Tagus give place. Let the vulgar herd set their hearts on dross if they will. For myself, let Apollo bestow on me cups overflowing with the waters of Castaly; let the myrtle that dreads the cold adorn my brow and let my verses ever be scanned by the eager lover. While we live we serve as food for Envy; when we are dead we rest within the aureole of the glory we have earned. So, when the funeral fires have consumed me, I shall live on, and the better part of me will have triumphed over death.

THE LOVES

BOOK II

ELEGY I

BEHOLD here another work of Ovid, who was born in
the moist land of the Peligni, of Ovid who singeth to
the world of his own follies. This time, again, 'twas Love
that willed it. Hence! Avaunt! ye prim and prudish ones.
No fitting audience, ye, to strains that sing of tender love.
I would be read of none save the maiden that grows warm
when she beholds her lover, and of the boy till now un-
visited by Love. I pray, too, that some young man, wounded
by an arrow sped from the same bow that hath stricken me,
may recognize in my verse the image of the flames whereby
he is consumed. Long may he marvel, and then at last exclaim, "How comes it that this poet singeth the very story
of my love? Who is it hath informed him?"

I was, I remember, making bold to sing of the Wars of
Heaven and Gyges of the hundred hands, and verily I was
well equipped for that great argument. I was about to sing
the fell revenge of Tellus and the fall of Pelion with Ossa
crashing down from high Olympus whereon they were em-
piled. In my hands I held the clouds, Jove and his thunderbolts, wherewith he would not have failed to defend his
heavenly realms. And then my mistress slammed her door
against me. Forthwith I dropped Jupiter and his lightnings;
aye, Jupiter himself clean vanished from my mind. Forgive
me, Jupiter; thy weapons were of no avail to me. That close-
shut door moved me more than all thy thunderbolts. Back

to my love songs and my gentle elegies went I; those are the arms for me, and ere long my gentle plaint moved to compassion the unfeeling doors. Poetry hath power to bring the blood-red moon to earth; poetry stayeth in mid-career the snow-white coursers of the sun. Poetry robbeth the serpent of his poisoned fang, and maketh the rivers to flow backward to their sources. Poetry hath battered down doors, it hath forced back locks, how tight soever they were welded to the massy oak. What had it booted me to sing Achilles fleet of foot; what would the sons of Atreus have done for me, or he who waged fierce war for ten long years and then wandered ten more upon his homeward way; or hapless Hector, dragged by the Hæmonian steeds across the dusty plain? But as soon as ever I pipe the praises of a sweet young girl, she cometh in person to pay the singer for his song. And that, methinks, is no small recompense. So farewell, ye heroes with illustrious names; not yours to bestow, the favors that I crave. But as for you, my charmers, look sweetly on the songs which rosy Cupid singeth in mine ear.

ELEGY II

TO THE EUNUCH BAGOAS, BEGGING HIM TO GIVE HIM ACCESS TO THE FAIR ONE COMMITTED TO HIS CHARGE

THOU, Bagoas, who art entrusted with the task of guarding thy mistress, lend me thine ear. I have but a couple of words to say to you, but they are weighty ones. Yesterday I saw a lady walking in the portico beneath the temple of Apollo. At once I fell in love with her and importuned her in writing. In answer, with a trembling hand, she wrote:

"Impossible." And why is it impossible? I asked. And she
replied that you keep too strict a watch on her.

Now listen to me, my over-watchful friend; if you are
wise you will give up getting yourself hated. If people fear
you, they will long for you to die. Her husband, too, is a
fool, for why be at such pains to guard a thing whereof, even
if you watch it not, no part is lost? Still, if he is madman
enough, let him indulge his passion to the full, and believe
her chaste who gives her charms to all. But for thee, vouchsafe her, in secret, a modicum of freedom. What you give
her in that direction she will repay. Just let her take you
into her confidence a little, and the mistress will do what the
slave shall bid. Afraid of conniving a little? Why, you've
only got to shut your eyes. Is she reading a letter in secret?
Well, take it that it's from her mother. A stranger comes
to call? Take him for some old acquaintance. She goes to
see a sick friend who isn't sick at all? Why, pretend she *is*
sick. Is she a long time coming? Let your head droop on
your breast, and snore away to your heart's content. Don't
go worrying your head about what they're doing in the temple of Isis, or what's going on in the theaters.

A discreet accomplice wins a deal of glory, and after all,
what is simpler than to hold your tongue? Such a man is
liked, he rules the household and never gets a beating. He
is a man of power; the others, scurvy fellows, merely slaves.
In order to keep the husband sweet, he stuffs him with fairy
tales and, masters both, they both approve of what delights
the woman. A husband may frown and furrow his brow
with wrinkles, a wheedling woman always gets her way.
Still, every now and then she must seem to have a grudge
against you, pretend to cry and say you are a brute. Your
cue is then to accuse her of some fault that she can readily
disprove. In taxing her with what is false, you blind her husband to the real truth. This if you do, honors and money

will be showered upon you. Act as I bid you, and you'll soon be a slave no more.

You see informers laden with heavy chains, you see false-hearted knaves shut up in gloomy dungeons. Tantalus is thirsty, with water all about him; surrounded by fruit, of fruit he cannot taste. That's all because he was a blabber. Because he gave too strict effect to Juno's bidding, Io's guard died ere his prime, and Io is a goddess.

I have seen a fellow loaded with chains that were making his legs black and blue, because he had insisted on telling a husband of his wife's amours. He merited a weightier doom; his prating tongue had killed the happiness of two. He filled the husband's heart with grief and slew his wife's good name.

Mark what I say; there never was a husband yet that liked such charges brought against his spouse. Hear them he may, but he'll never hear them with pleasure. If he be indifferent, all your precious tale is wasted; if he love her, then 'tis you who kill his peace of mind. Nay, howsoever clear a woman's fault may be, it takes a deal of proving. The judge's sympathies are all for her. Even if he had seen the whole thing with his own eyes, he would still believe her, if she denied it. He would say his eyes deceived him; that he himself had been at fault. Let her but fall a-weeping, he'll mingle his tears with hers and say, "This babbling ass shall get it hot for this." You see, the odds are nearly all against you, and if you lose, you get a thrashing, while she's being dandled on the judge's knee.

It is no crime we meditate. It is not to mix a poisoned draught that we desire to meet. No naked dagger flashes in our hand. All we ask is that, by your good offices, we may love in safety; and what request could be more innocent than that?

ELEGY III

HE APPEALS ONCE MORE TO BAGOAS, WHO HAD PROVED INFLEXIBLE

AH me, that my mistress should be entrusted to thy care, thou who art nor man nor woman, thou who can'st never know the mutual joy that lovers give—and take. He who was the first to rob little boys of that which makes a man, deserved, himself, to suffer a like fate. Thou wouldst be less unbending, thou wouldst incline more willingly thine ear to my request, if ever thou hadst loved a woman. Thou art not made to mount the fiery steed, to handle heavy arms, or, in thy right hand, wield the warlike spear. It needs a man for that; and to do aught manly thou must never hope. Follow no standard but the standard of thy mistress. 'Tis she that thou must wait on hand and foot; make the most of her favors. If thou lose her, what purpose wilt thou serve? Her face, her youth invite to dalliance. 'Twere ill her loveliness should fade and perish in base neglect. She may have hoodwinked thee, however troublesome thou may'st appear. What lovers want, they'll find the means to get; but since, perhaps, 'twere best to see what prayers will do, we do entreat you now, while yet there's time, to give our prayers effect.

ELEGY IV

HE CONFESSES HIS INCLINATION FOR LOVE AND HIS ADMIRATION FOR ALL MANNER OF WOMEN

I MAKE no pretense of justifying the laxity of my morals; I never resort to untruthful pretexts to excuse my wanderings from the path of virtue. I freely confess my faults, if such avowals can serve any useful purpose. Now I have acknowledged my guilt in general terms, I mean to make a clean breast of all my follies. I curse my failings, yet I cannot help finding pleasure in the very faults that I deplore. How burdensome is the yoke that one would fain cast off. I have not the strength nor the will-power to govern my passions; they bear me along with them, even as the swift tide hurries away the slender bark.

It is not any particular type of beauty that sets my heart on fire. A hundred motives compel me to be always in love. Here is a girl that drops her gaze demurely. That is enough, my heart catches fire and her modesty is the lure that ensnares me. And here is one that is out for booty. To her I fall a willing victim because she is no novice and because she bids fair to be keen and enterprising on a downy couch. And then, if I see one with an expression that recalls to me the Sabine dames, I forthwith tell myself that she has longings but knows how to conceal them. Are you a learned lady? I fall in love with your rare accomplishments. Unlearned? Your *naïveté* enthralls me. This one finds Callimachus a sorry poet compared with me. I please her, and lo, straightway she pleases me. This one finds fault with my verses and tells me I am no poet. Despite her strictures I fain would have her in my arms. This one walks languorously. Her gait enchants me. This one is prim. Peradven-

ture, if she had a lover 'twould soften her. This one sings delightfully, and breathes from her soft throat the most melodious strains. I long to steal a kiss from her parted lips. Another lightly fingers the trembling chords of her lyre; where is he who could help adoring such skillful fingers? Here is one that wins me with her dancing. I feast my eyes on her seductive poses, on the rhythmic movements of her arms, on the swaying of her whole body as she moves in time to the music. But never mind me, whom any one can set on fire. Let Hippolytus see her; even he would become a Priapus. You, my tall beauty, recall the heroines of olden days and the bed is not a whit too long for you. And you, my dainty little treasure; I love you, too, just as much. Both are enchanting. Tall and short, I love them both. Here is one that wears no finery; I muse how jewels would enhance her beauty. Here is one tricked out with gems; how dazzling are her charms. Of fair and dark I am alike the slave; white-skinned or sunburnt, I adore them all. Black tresses flutter on a snowy neck? Leda's loveliness lay in her raven hair. Is she fair, the girl I see yonder? Why, 'twas to her golden hair Aurora owed her beauty. Everywhere history helps me to justify my love. A young woman delights me, an older one enthralls me. The one has the beauty of her body, the other experience and richness of mind, to recommend her. In a word, of all the beauties they rave about in Rome, there's none whose lover I am not fain to be.

ELEGY V

HE UPBRAIDS HIS MISTRESS WHOM HE HAS DETECTED
ACTING FALSELY TOWARDS HIM

AWAY with thee, Cupid and thy quiver! Love's not such a priceless thing that I should so often and so desperately long for death. Aye, for death I long, when I bethink me of thy perfidy, thou thankless girl, born to be a lasting grief to me. 'Tis not thy tablets carelessly effaced that reveal thy conduct to me; 'tis not the presents secretly received that tell me thy misdeeds. Would to heaven I could fail to prove the accusation that I bring against thee. Ah, hapless me, why is my cause so good! Happy the lover who can boldly defend the woman he adores; happy he to whom his mistress may say, "Free of all guilt am I!" Hard of heart is he, and too indulgent of his grief, who would seek to win a sanguinary triumph by bringing home a crime to the woman that he loves.

Alas, I saw it all when you thought I was asleep. Aye, with these eyes did I behold your treason, for the wine beside me had not dulled my vision. I saw you making eyes at him, I saw your nods of the head, and read it all as plainly as if it had been written down in words. Your eyes were not silent; I saw letters writ in wine upon the table, even thy fingers had their tale to tell. Try as you would to hide it, I read the meaning of your discourse, and guessed the cipher of your secret code. And now the throng of guests had left the table and only two remained, both young, both drunk with wine. And then I saw you both exchange most wanton kisses, kisses in which, as I too plainly saw, your tongues were intermingled. Not such kisses as a sister gives her sober-minded brother, but such as a loving mistress might bestow upon her eager lover; not such kisses as Phœbus to Diana gives, but such, we may believe, as Venus often lavished on her darling Mars.

"How now!" cried I. "On whom dost thou bestow the favors that are mine? Nay, these things are mine by right. My right I'll hold, my right I will defend. Thy kisses are for me and mine for thee, alone. What does this interloper, then, coming between us twain?"

In such-like words did I outpour my grief. The blush of shame o'erspread her guilty cheeks. So flushes the eastern sky when Tithonus' spouse arises from his bed, and so doth blush the maiden when her betrothed resteth his gaze upon her. So roses shine when lilies round them blow; so turns the pale moon red when by some magic spell her course in heaven is stayed; so gleams Assyrian ivory that a Mæonian dame has dyed with crimson so that it may not yellow grow with years. Such then, or as near as may be, was the color of the wench's cheeks, and never had I seen her look more lovely. She looked on the ground; the look became her. Sad was her countenance; the sadness suited her. Her hair, and deftly was it braided, I nearly tore out by the roots. Her dainty cheeks, I all but laid rude hands upon. But when I saw her face, my arms fell strengthless at my side; by weapons of her own was my mistress defended. I who a moment since she had seen so fierce and menacing, now cast myself at her feet and begged her to give me kisses no less tender. She smiled, and then, with all her heart and soul, gave me a kiss, and never was kiss more sweet. 'Twas such a kiss as would have filched the thunderbolt from the hand of angry Jove. Yet how my breast is tortured now, lest another may have tasted kisses just as sweet; I hope that those were not of this celestial quality. These last kisses that she gave me were better far than those which I had taught her; she hath, methinks, acquired some novel art. It bodes no good, this too, too luscious sweetness; it bodes no good that all your tongue within my mouth was thrust, all mine within your own. And 'tis not this alone that grieves me; not only of these voluptuous kisses that I complain, albeit complain I do, but what rankles most is the thought that lessons such as those could have been given nowhere but in bed, and I know not who is the instructor that has received such rich remuneration.

ELEGY VI

HE LAMENTS THE DEATH OF THE PARROT HE HAD GIVEN TO HIS MISTRESS

OUR parrot, winged mimic of the human voice, sent from farthest Ind, is dead. Come ye in flocks, ye birds, unto his obsequies. Come, ye pious denizens of the air; beat your bosoms with your wings and with your rigid claws, score furrows on your dainty heads. Even as mourners rend their hair, rend ye your ruffled plumes. Since the far-sounding clarion is silent, sing ye a doleful song. Wherefore, O Philomel, mourn ye the dark deed of the Ismarian tyrant? Time should have ended that lament. Keep it to mourn for the passing of the rarest of thy kind. The fate of Itys was once a mighty theme of sorrow; but all that was long ago. All ye who float with outspread wings in the liquid air, and thou before all others, loving turtle, breathe forth your mournful plaint. He was, all his life long, a faithful friend to thee and never did he waver in his loyalty. What young Pylades the Phocian was to Argive Orestes, such, my parrot, was the turtle-dove to thee, so long as thou didst live.

But how did this fidelity bestead thee, and what availed the brilliant colors of thy plumage rare? or that voice so skilled in mimicking the tones of human speech? What did it boot thee to win the affection of my mistress from the very moment thou wast given her? O hapless one, thou wast the glory of birds, and now thou art no more! With thy wondrous plumage, thou couldst outshine the green fire of the emerald, and the hue of thy beak was of the richest red. No bird on earth could speak so well as thou, so great thy skill in imitating, with thy nasal tones, the sounds that thou hadst heard.

Now envious death hath stricken thee; never wast thou at war with any bird. Thou wast garrulous and didst love the piping times of peace. See, the quails are for ever at war; that, perchance, is why they live so long. Thou didst ask for very little; and sith you loved so much to gossip, your beak had very little time for food. A nut was all thy dinner, a poppy-seed or two would bring thee sleep, and with a sip of water thou wouldst quench thy thirst. The hungry vulture lives, and the kite that weaves his circles in the air, and the rain-foretelling daw. The raven, whom the panoplied Minerva hates, lives on—nine generations will hardly see it die. But he is dead, this bird, this babbling echo of the human voice, this gift so rare brought from the utmost limits of the world. 'Tis nearly always so; the greedy hands of death strike first at what is best upon the earth, and things of little worth accomplish to the full their destined tale of years. Thersites beheld the melancholy obsequies of Protesilaus; Hector came to dust and ashes while yet his brothers lived.

What boots it to recall how, with fear at her breast, my mistress prayed for thee—prayers caught up by the swift-wingèd South and carried o'er the seas? The seventh day had come, the seventh, and thy last. Fate had unwound thy thread of days. Howbeit even then thou spakest, crying, with thy dying breath, "Corinna, fare thee well!"

There, in Elysium, on a hill-side's gentle slope there stands a forest of broad, shady oaks, and over the moist soil the rich grass spreads its coverlet of green. Here, if the fabled tale we may believe, abide all innocent birds, and here no fowl of evil omen ever comes. Here range the harmless swans, and here the one undying Phœnix dwells. Here doth the peacock proudly show his gorgeous plumage and the crooning dove showers kisses on her eager mate. Here in their midst, here in these pleasant woody places, our parrot speaks and calls around him all birds of gentle soul. His bones a mound doth cover, a little mound as doth befit his size, and on it is a little stone that bears this little legend:

> From this memorial, you may see
> What love my mistress bore to me.
> Whene'er to her I spake, my words
> Meant more than any other bird's.

ELEGY VII

HE ASSURES CORINNA THAT HE HAS NEVER HAD ANY GUILTY COMMERCE WITH CYPASSIS, HER MAID

OH, are you always going to be bringing some fresh charge against me? No sooner have I succeeded in rebutting one than you trump up another. I'm sick of this perpetual bickering. If I happen to run my eye along the topmost tier of the theater, you'll be sure to pick one woman out of the crowd there and make her a pretext for some more nagging. If a woman merely glances in my direction, and I don't look back at her, my indifference, you'll say, is all put on; there's something between us right enough. If I say anything nice about a woman, you immediately start tearing your hair; if I say anything nasty, well, you say it's just a blind. If I'm looking well, it's because I leave you

alone; and if I'm not, I'm dying of love for some one else.
I shouldn't so much mind if I had really done something.
It's easier to put up with troubles you've brought on yourself; but you upbraid me without rime or reason, and your
fatal proclivity for believing the worst about everybody,
weakens whatever effect your fulminations might otherwise
have had. Look at that poor old long-eared donkey there;
he doesn't mend his pace, for all their whackings.

And now you've got another grievance. It's your smart
little maid, Cypassis, with whom I am supposed to have mis-
conducted myself this time, is it? And in your bed, too.
Now if ever I feel inclined to go astray, the gods forbid that
I should do so with a servant-girl. What man would ever
willingly have relations with a slave or want to fondle a
back all covered with weals? And, mark you, this particular
slave is the one that gives the finishing touches to your hair,
whose clever fingers make you look so irresistible; and I am
supposed to go philandering with some one who thinks there's
not a woman like you in the world? Is it likely? I should
only get snubbed for my pains, and she'd tell you all about
it. No, I swear by Venus and by the bow of her wingèd
boy, I'm innocent of the charge you bring against me.

ELEGY VIII

HE ASKS CYPASSIS HOW IN THE WORLD CORINNA
COULD HAVE FOUND THEM OUT

YOU wonderful little hair-dresser, who only ought to have
goddesses' hair to tend, Cypassis, whom in a stolen moment of delight I found by no means unexpert, you who
suit your mistress so well, and me better still, tell me who
has given our secret away? How did Corinna get wind of

our clandestine delights? Did I turn red? Did I let fall a single word that could have betrayed our hidden pleasures? Nay, didn't I swear that for a man to hanker after a servant-girl he couldn't have all his wits about him.

And yet the Thessalian hero burned with desire for the lovely Briseis, and she was but a slave. No more than a slave was she, the priestess that cast her lures about the King of Mycenæ. Am I then greater than Achilles, greater than the son of Tantalus? Shall I blush at what was deemed a fitting portion for a king?

Nevertheless, when she turned that angry look upon you, I saw you blush red all over. I was not anything like so flustered. I, if you remember, swore by great Venus herself that I was innocent. But you, my goddess, ordain that this beneficent lie may be swept by the warm South over the Carpathian deep.

In payment for these my services, my dusky Cypassis, grant me the sweet pleasure of lying with you to-day. Why do you say no? Why, ungrateful girl, why pretend you are afraid? It will be enough to have deserved well of one of your masters. If you are silly enough to refuse, I shall confess all we have done. I shall become my own accuser, and I shall tell your mistress—yes, I shall, Cypassis—where and how often we have met, what we did, in how many ways, and what they were.

ELEGY IX

HE BESEECHES CUPID NOT TO DISCHARGE ALL HIS ARROWS AT HIM ALONE

O THOU who dost never weary of tormenting me, who never givest me any peace of mind, why, Cupid, dost thou treat me thus, who never ceased to march beneath thy banner? Why dost thou wound me thus? Why scorchest thou thine own friends with that torch of thine; why doth thy bow transfix them with its shafts? 'Twere better thou should'st prove thy might on one who resisteth thee. Did not the hero of Hæmonia, after piercing Telephus with his spear, heal with that same spear the wound that he had made? The huntsman chaseth the quarry that flees before him, yet once he hath seized it, he setteth it at liberty, and hasteneth after a fresh prey. 'Tis for us, thy loyal followers, that thou dost keep thy weapons, albeit thy sluggish arm smiteth not the foe that resisteth. Wherefore spend thine arrows on these fleshless bones? For in truth Love hath left me nought but skin and bones. Loveless live so many maidens, so many youths know nought of love. Over these, then, should be thy victory.

Rome, had she not extended her might throughout the world, would be to-day nought but a huddled group of straw-thatched huts. The war-worn veteran lays down his arms and tills his allotted fields. The courser, freed from his stall, leapeth in the meadow; vast docks shelter the vessel that hath returned to port, and the gladiator yieldeth up his weapons for the wand that quits him of his toils. And I who have fought so many campaigns in Love's service, is it not time that I should live in peace?

Yet if some god should come to me and say, "Henceforth

thou shalt live a loveless life," I should demur to his decree, so sweet a plague is woman. When I have had my fill of love, when I feel its fires no more, I am driven I know not whither by an indescribable tumult of the mind. Just as the horseman, tugging vainly at the foam-flecked bridle, sees himself hurried to the abyss's edge; just as the pinnace, nearing the shore and about to bound into port, is suddenly carried out to sea again by a gust of wind; so am I blown hither and thither by Cupid's changeful breath, and Love of the rosy cheeks makes me once more the target for his arrows.

Shoot on, my little one! I have laid down my arms; naked I stand, shoot on! Here show off thy strength; here display thy skill. Here in this spot, without awaiting thy command, thy arrows come and bury themselves; the quiver is scarcely more familiar to them than is my heart.

Foul fall the man who can slumber the whole night through and thinks so much of sleep. Fool! What is sleep but the image of cold Death. Thou shalt sleep long enough one of these days.

As for me, I would that my mistress should sometimes cheat me with lying promises. The anticipation of bliss I hold to be a boon in itself; I would have her sometimes caress, sometimes upbraid me. I like her to surrender often, and often to resist. If Mars is inconstant, Cupid, 'tis thanks to thee. Yea, 'tis after thy example that thy mother's lover bears his arms now here, now there. Thou art fickle, far lighter than thy wings, and as the fancy takes thee, thou givest and withholdest the delights of love. Howbeit if thou and thy gracious mother will but hearken to my prayers, thou wilt come and reign in my heart and never quit it more. May all the too-inconstant host of fair ones rally to my banner. Thus of both sexes at once shalt thou adorèd be.

ELEGY X

HE TELLS GRÆCINUS HOW, DESPITE WHAT HE SAYS TO
THE CONTRARY, IT IS POSSIBLE TO BE IN LOVE
WITH TWO WOMEN AT THE SAME TIME

'TWAS thou, oh, yes, I mind me well, 'twas thou,
Græcinus, who wast wont to say a man could never
love two women at a time. 'Tis, then, through thee that I
have been deceived, through thee that, all defenseless and
unarmed, I've fallen into the snare, for here in me—oh,
scoundrel that I am—thou dost behold a man in love with
two fair charmers at a time. Lovely are both and both in
love with dress. In artifice I scarcely know which one the
other doth surpass. Now doth the first the second one outshine, and now the second doth eclipse the first; yes, sometimes one, and then, anon, the other, taketh my fancy most.
My heart, like to a barque tossed by opposing winds, veers
sometimes hither, sometimes thither, between these rival loves.
Oh, wherefore, Erycina, wherefore dost thou everlastingly
increase my torments. Did not one mistress suffice to keep
me busy? Wherefore to the trees add leaves, stars to the
starry sky, or water to the boundless deep?

Howbeit 'twere better so, than live a loveless life. The
life that scorns delights and lives laborious days I'll leave my
enemies. Let them sleep soundly in their lonely beds, lie in
the middle and stretch themselves to their heart's content.
As for myself, I'd liefer cruel love should break my downy
slumbers; I would not be my bed's sole burden, no, not I.
Let my mistress, without let or hindrance, ease me of love's
pangs if she alone be equal to the task. If she be not, then
I'll have two of them. My body's thin, but strong; it lacks
not strength, but flesh. Besides, Love's joys my prowess will

sustain. Never a woman have I disappointed yet, and often after battling all the night, the morn hath found me ready to renew the fray. Happy he who dies in the lists of Love. I pray the gods that such may be my end. The soldier, if he will, may oppose his breast to the foeman's spears, and buy undying glory with his blood. The miser may roam the world in search of wealth, and when he's ship-wrecked, let his lying mouth choke with the seas his vessel's keel hath plowed. Be it *my* lot softly to fade away doing Love's service, to die in the very crisis of the fray. And may some gentle soul, shedding a tear upon my grave, exclaim "in sooth thy death did well become thy life."

ELEGY XI

HE SEEKS TO DISSUADE CORINNA FROM GOING TO BAIÆ

YES, it was the ship of pine hewn on Mount Pelion, that first opened a path over the wonder-stricken billows— a path beset with perils and bestrewn with reefs—the ship of pine which, amid the clashing rocks, bore away the ram famed for its golden fleece. Would to heaven that the Argo had been swallowed up in the depths of the sea so that never mortal man should vex the wide ocean with his oars. For see now, here is Corinna leaving her own dear bed and all her household gods, and making ready to trust herself to the deceiving deep. Wherefore dost thou make thy hapless lover tremble for thy sake at every wind that blows, the West wind and the East, the icy North and the warm South? Thou'lt find no cities on thy way, no woods to enchant thy gaze, only and always the blue-gray waters of the treacherous main. Not on the open sea wilt thou discover dainty shells and pebbles many-hued; they are the pastime of the

sandy shore; leave on the sands, my sweet ones, the imprint
of your lovely feet; there doth safety lie; beyond, who knows
what perils lurk? Let others tell thee of the warring winds,
what seas by Scylla and Charybdis are infested, and on what
rocks enthroned the grim Ceraunian peaks tower o'er the
main, and where the Syrtes hidden lie, where Malea lurks.
These things let others tell. Whate'er they say, give credence
to their tales; for tempests the believer never harm. When
once the cable's loosed and the carven ship sweeps out on to
the wide, salt sea, 'tis long ere one beholds the land again.
Then doth the anxious sailor dread the wrath of the winds
and sees the face of death in every wave. What will become
of you if Triton stirs his waves to fury. You'll look a pretty
pallid object then. Then you'll cry for succor to the sons
of fruitful Leda and exclaim, "Happy the woman that's safe
on her native shore." It's a far safer thing to snuggle down
in bed, to read diverting tales, or wake the music of the
Thracian lyre. But if my words be vain and wind-dispersed,
may Galatea look with favor on thy ship. If so precious and
so fair a freight were lost, heavy on you, daughters divine
of Nereus, heavy on thee, old Nereus thyself, would lie the
blame. Go then, and take me with thee in thy thoughts;
go thou, and soon return with prospering gales, and stronger
be the winds that on thy homeward way shall swell thy sails.
Let mighty Nereus roll the billows toward these shores, let
all the winds breathe hither, and hither let the moon the
waters draw. Pray thou thyself the Zephyrs to breathe full
upon thy sails, and with thine own hand shake the canvas out.

I, gazing seawards from the shore, shall be the first to see
thy vessel dear, and I shall cry, "That barque brings home
my heaven." I'll fold thee in my arms, and with a riot of
wild kisses smother thee; the victim, consecrate to thy return,
shall slaughtered be; the sands of the shore I'll fashion like

a couch, and any mound will serve us for a table. There, with the wine beside us, thou shalt all thy tale narrate; thou shalt tell me how thy vessel almost foundered mid the waves; thou shalt tell how, in hastening home to me, thou didst not fear the cold, dark nights, no, nor the stormy southern gales. They may be travelers' tales, yet I'll believe them, every one. Wherefore should I not smile on what I long for most? Oh, may the Morning Star, that has no rival in the fields of night, spur on his steed and bring with speed that happy day.

ELEGY XII

HE REJOICES AT HAVING AT LAST WON THE FAVORS OF CORINNA

COME, bind ye my brows, ye laurels of victory, for I have conquered; lo, in my arms I hold her, this wonderful Corinna, whom husband, watchman, oaken door and all such enemies to love, were guarding from the invader. This is a victory specially deserving of triumphal honors, since the prize, without bloodshed, has been gained. No lowly ramparts, nor towns with narrow moats begirt, but a woman it is that my generalship has won.

When, after twice five years of war, Troy fell, what, among so many claimants for reward, was the prize that fell to Atreus' son? But now, the glory of the day is mine and mine alone; no other can demand his share of the spoils. I was the leader, I the host, that took the citadel by storm. Cavalry, infantry and standard-bearer I. By no mischance did Fortune mar my feats. A Triumph then for me, the guerdon of my efforts! The cause of my campaign is no new thing. Had not the daughter of Tyndarus been carried off, the peace of Europe and of Asia had not been dis-

turbed. 'Twas a woman who, when the wine was going the
rounds, stirred up to mutual strife the fierce Lapithæ and
the monstrous race of the Centaurs. 'Twas a woman who,
in thy kingdom, good Latinus, forced the Trojans to begin
fresh wars; 'twas woman who, when the City was but newly
founded, did cause the bloody conflict when the Romans
had to battle with the fathers of their wives. Bulls I have
seen fighting for a snow-white heifer, which, looking on at
the fray, stirred them to fresh exploits. Me too, as others
oft before me, hath Cupid bidden march to battle under his
banners, but mine was a bloodless victory.

ELEGY XIII

HE BESEECHES ISIS TO COME TO THE AID OF CORINNA IN HER CONFINEMENT

MY rash Corinna, seeking to rid herself of the burden she
bears in her womb, hath risked the loss of her own
life. For having thus, unknown to me, courted so great a
danger, she merits all my wrath; but wrath gives way to
fear. Howbeit it was by me that she conceived, or such, at
least, is my belief; for oftentimes my facts are only perad-
ventures.

Isis, thou who in Parætonium dost dwell, and in Canopus'
kindly meads and Memphis and palm-bearing Pharos and
those plains where the Nile, quitting its mighty bed, flows
and bears through seven channels its hurrying waters to the
sea. By thy timbrels I entreat thee, and by the head of
dread Anubis—so may the pious Osiris ever accept thy offerings, so may the drowsy serpent glide round about thine
altars, and the hornèd Apis march in the procession; look
mercifully on Corinna, and spare two lives in one, for thou

to my mistress wilt give life; she will give life to me. Full often, on days appointed for thy worship, hath she sat within thy temple at the hour when thy priests enwreathe their brows with laurel.

And thou who takest pity on women who are suffering the pangs of childbirth when they seek to be delivered of the burden that stirs within them, come, propitious Ilithyia, and hearken to my prayers. She merits that thou shouldst count her among thy favored ones; and I, appareled all in white, will offer incense at thine altars. I at thy feet will lay my votive gifts, and this inscription will I add: "Ovid for Corinna's safety makes this offering." And all I pray thee is to justify these same offerings and inscription.

And as for thee, Corinna, if, in my panic, I may give thee such advice, I'll say to thee, once safely out of the wood this time, take heed thou enter not again therein.

ELEGY XIV

ON CORINNA'S RECOVERY HE WRITES TO HER AGAIN CONCERNING HER ATTEMPT AT ABORTION AND TELLS HER HOW NAUGHTY SHE HAS BEEN

WHAT avails it that our women should be free from the perils of the field, that they should not be called upon, buckler in hand, to march with our doughty troops if, though far from the dangers of war, they wound themselves with their own shafts and with rash hands seek to compass their own destruction? She who first essayed to expel from her womb the tender fruit she bore therein, deserved to perish in the struggle she had invited. What, to avoid a few wrinkles on thy stomach, must the sand be strewed for a veritable scene of carnage?

If in the childhood of the world mothers had followed this wicked custom, the human race would have vanished from the face of the earth, and to re-people the world by sowing those stones whence our ancestors were born, a second Deucalion had been required. Who would have overthrown the kingdom of Priam if Thetis, goddess of the seas, had not been willing to bear her fruit until the term allotted by nature? If Ilia had smothered the twins she bore within her, the founder of the ruling city of the world would never have been born. If Venus had slain Æneas in the womb, the earth would have been bereft of the Cæsars. And thou, who wast born so fair, wouldst have perished had thy mother done that act thou hast just essayed. And I, who am more fitted to die of love, would never have existed.

Wherefore despoil the fruitful vine of the swelling grape? Wherefore, with cruel hand, tear away the fruit ere it be ripe? When ripe it will drop of its own accord, and once 'tis borne, let it increase at will; to bring new life into the world is meet reward for a few months of patience.

O women, why will ye desecrate your entrails with the instruments of death? Why offer dread poisons to infants yet unborn? We curse the Colchian damsel spattered with the blood of her own children; we bewail the fate of Itys, slain by her own mother. Aye, these were fell and cruel women; but their cruelty had its motive. Each took vengeance on her husband by shedding his children's blood. Tell me, then, what Tereus, what Jason prompts you to rend your body with such desperate hand?

The Armenian tigresses behave not thus, nor dares the lioness destroy an offspring of her own. Such acts by dainty women are performed, yet not always with impunity. Many a time she slays herself who slays her offspring in the womb. She dies herself and with disheveled hair is borne away upon her bed of anguish, and all who see her cry, "Well was her doom deserved."

But let my empty words be borne away on the wind; let my forebodings all be vain. Ye gods, be kind to her and punish not Corinna for her first misdeed. 'Tis all I ask; let your chastisement be reserved for her second lapse.

ELEGY XV

TO THE RING WHICH HE IS SENDING TO HIS MISTRESS

O LITTLE ring that art going to encircle my fair mistress's finger, thou that no value hast save the giver's love that goes with thee, be charming in her sight. May she with delight receive thee and straightway slip thee on her finger. May thou fit her, as well as she fits me; and may thy circle, nor over-tight nor yet too loose, softly gird her finger.

Happy ring, thou wilt be touched by her I love. Ah me, already I begin to envy my own gift's happy lot. Would that the enchantress of the Ææan Isle or the Old Man of Carpathos would change me to a ring. Then, lady, I should wish that you should touch thy breasts and slip thy left hand underneath thy tunic. Off from your finger I should glide, however tight and clinging. As by some wizard's art, would I grow loose and slip into your bosom. Aye, and when she would seal her secret missives, so that the wax should not cling to the dry stone, I first should touch my fair mistress's moist lips, so only that I might never seal a word that would to myself bring grief. If she were fain to lay me in the casket, I'd refuse to leave her finger. I'd small and smaller grow so as to clip her the more closely. Never, my love, my life, may I give thee cause to blush for me, or grow too heavy

for thy dainty finger. Wear me e'en when you take your
bath, nor fear the water will unloose the gem. And yet,
methinks, if naked I beheld thee, I should be consumed with
desire, and that ring would like a man acquit itself.

Ah me! Why do I long for things that cannot be? Go
forth, little gift, upon thy way, and may my mistress see in
thee the symbol of my changeless love.

ELEGY XVI

TO CORINNA, BESEECHING HER TO VISIT HIM IN HIS COUNTRY HOME AT SULMO

BEHOLD me at Sulmo, in the land of the Peligni. It is
a little spot, but bright and clean with its streams of
sparkling water. Though the scorching sun may crack the
earth, though the Dog Star shine his fiercest, limpid stream-
lets wind their way across the fields of the Peligni and there
the grass is always green. The land with corn is rich, and
with the vine is richer still. The olive, too, flourishes in
profusion on this light, loose soil. The rivulets meandering
among the meadows clothe the moist earth with shadowy
verdure.

But there my love is not. Or stay—my love is there, but
not the object of my love. Nay, if betwixt Castor and
Pollux you should set me, I would not dwell in heaven itself
without you.

Let death be bitter and let the earth lie heavy upon them,
who first drave their roads into the far-off regions of the
earth. At least they should have bidden their mistresses go
with them, if indeed they were compelled to furrow the
world with their interminable tracks. So, even if I, benumbed with cold, had had to cross the wind-swept Alps,

that journey, painful though it be, would have been sweet to me, if only my love had borne me company. With my mistress at my side, the Libyan quicksands I would boldly cross, and spread my canvas to the treacherous southern gales; with her beside me, I'd not fear the monsters that yelp at Scylla's side, nor yet thy narrow straits, O tortuous Malea, no, nor the waters which the unwearying Charybdis, sated with sunken wrecks, spews forth and swallows up again.

But if the might of the winds prevail, if the billows bear away the gods who would fain come to our assistance, fling thou thy snowy arms about my neck and freely the sweet burden will I sustain. Many a time and oft, to behold his Hero, Leander swam the straits; nor would he have perished, had not the darkness blotted out the distance from his sight.

Here, of my darling one bereft, though I gaze upon rich vineyards, on fields watered with limpid streams, though I behold the river, at the husbandman's behest, unraveling itself in many channels, and see the leaves of the trees lightly stirred by cooling breezes, I seem not to be dwelling in the fair land of the Pelignians; nor in the familiar home of my ancestors, the place which saw my birth. Nay, I seem to be in the heart of Scythia, or among the grim Cilicians, or the Britons who paint themselves with green, or the rocks red with the blood of Prometheus.

The elm loves the vine, the vine clings to the elm; why, then, am I so often sundered from my mistress? And yet thou shouldst never leave me, for thou wast wont to swear, both by myself and by your eyes, my stars, that thou wouldst never quit my side. Lighter than autumn leaves, the empty promises of woman are whirled away and scattered on the bosom of the winds and the waters.

Howbeit, if thou hast any pity for me in my lonely state, begin to make thy words bear fruit in deeds. Quick, up with you into your little chaise, and with your own hands shake the reins about your horses' flying manes. And you, ye swelling hills, abase yourselves before her as she comes; ye paths in the winding vales, be smooth beneath her feet.

ELEGY XVII

HE COMPLAINS TO CORINNA THAT SHE IS TOO CONCEITED ABOUT HER GOOD LOOKS

IF any one deems it a disgrace to be the slave of a beautiful woman, well then, I will plead guilty to the charge. Let him declare me an infamous fellow if he will, only let the goddess who rules over Paphos and wave-girt Cythera treat me a little more gently. Ah, would that I had fallen captive to a sweet and gentle woman, since I was fated to fall to a lovely one. Beauty engenders pride. Corinna is so fair, there's no managing her. Poor devil that I am, would she did not know how lovely she is! It is her mirror that makes her so conceited, and she never looks in it until her toilet is complete. Even if your charms do make you proud and promise conquests, charms that were born to captivate my eyes, that is no reason why you should treat me with disdain. High and low may mate together. They tell that the nymph Calypso, fired with love for a mortal, made him tarry with her against his will. 'Tis well known, too, that a daughter of Nereus did not disdain to lie with the King of Phthia, Egeria with Numa the Just, and Venus with Vulcan, limping withal and dirty as he came straight from his forge. These lines are not of equal length, yet the heroic meter matches well its shorter fellow.

Dear heart, take me on whatsoever terms thou wilt. Throned high upon thy bed, be pleased to let me know thy laws. I'll never raise an accusing finger at you; you'll never have to disavow our love.

Let my verses be to you instead of riches. More than one woman owes her fame to me. I know of one who everywhere gives out that she's Corinna. What would she not give to be Corinna in very sooth? But even as we see not the cool Eurotas and the poplar-fringed Po gliding along between the self-same banks, so none but thou shalt be the subject of my song, and thou alone shalt be my inspiration.

ELEGY XVIII

TO MACER: TO WHOM HE EXCUSES HIMSELF FOR GIVING HIMSELF UP WHOLLY TO EROTIC VERSE

WHILST in your verse you are depicting the wrath of Achilles, and are investing with their first arms the heroes who are bound by their oaths, I, Macer, am tasting the sweets of repose in the shade of Venus, and tender love restrains the daring flight of my genius. More than once I have said to my mistress, "Enough of this, now go thy ways." And forthwith she would seat herself on my knees. Often I have said to her, "Verily, I grow ashamed," and she, scarce able to restrain her tears, would cry, "Oh, hapless me! Art thou ashamed of me already?" Then, flinging her arms about me, she would shower kisses upon me, kisses that are my undoing. Then it is all over with me. My mind is occupied with anything but fighting. The things I sing are deeds performed within four walls, my private wars.

Howbeit I have handled the scepter; high tragic themes my pen has dared essay, nor did my powers prove too weak for that emprise. But Love did laugh to see my splendid cloak, my painted buskin and my scepter wielded with such address by hands ne'er made to grasp it. Again did my mistress' needs drag me from these labors, and the buskined poet by Cupid was undone.

Since, then, it is my lot, the art of love I'll sing and try no other themes. Behold I am urged on amain by the force of my own precepts. Either I tell what Penelope wrote to Ulysses or paint thy tears, Phyllis, when thou knewest thyself abandoned. I write to Paris and to Macareus, to the churlish Jason, to the father of Hippolytus, to Hippolytus himself. I sing the lamentations of the hapless Dido, armed with her threatening sword; I sing the sighs of the Lesbian heroine that loved the Aonian lyre.

With what speed has my friend Sabinus hastened o'er the world and brought from countless divers places the answer to these letters! The chaste Penelope recognized Ulysses' seal, and the step-mother of Hippolytus hath scanned the reproaches which he addresses to her. Jason's sad adieux have reached Hypsipyle, and Sapho, lover of Apollo, has but to lay at the feet of the god the lyre which she consecrated to him.

But you, too, Macer, who sing of battles and the deeds of Mars, you, too, have told, so far as thy task allowed, of love and its treasures. Paris in thy poem hath a place, and the fair adulteress whose crime made such a bruit in the world, and Laodamia, who quitted not her slaughtered lord. If I know thee well, thou treatest of these subjects as freely as thou singest of battles, and from thine own camp often strayest into mine.

ELEGY XIX

TO A MAN WITH WHOSE WIFE HE WAS IN LOVE

FOOL, if you don't want to keep an eye on your wife for your own sake, at least do so for mine, that it may whet my desire for her. What we can have for the asking we never want; to forbid a thing adds ardor to our longing.

He must have a heart like iron, who loves a woman he is free to love. As for us, who are versed in the art, we must have our hopes and fears, and we must have a few rebuffs to give zest to our appetite.

I don't want to hear about the happiness that never deceives. None of your steady-going, placid loves for me. My mistress must have something of the devil in her. That's a weakness of mine, and that, Corinna, cunning little minx, knew perfectly well. She knew only too thoroughly how to take me in her snare. How often, alas, have I known her, the lying jade, to say she had a dreadful headache, so as to keep me at arm's length, and how many times have I, despite the pangs it cost me, ruefully taken my departure. How many a time has she upbraided me, playing the injured innocent, when all the time it was she herself that was at fault. And when she had sufficiently tormented me, when she had revived the dying embers of my passion, she would relent and pander to my longings. How she would twine her arms about me, what loving words she'd lavish on me. How she would smother me with kisses, and, oh, ye gods, what luscious ones they were!

And thou, who just now charmed my vision, do thou too be cunning; turn often a deaf ear to my entreaties; suffer me, lying at thy door, to endure the biting cold of a long winter's night. 'Tis the only way to make my love endure.

'Tis that that's needed, 'tis that that adds fuel to my passion. For me a plain straightforward love-affair's devoid of savor. 'Tis like a dish with too much sugar in it. My gorge doth rise at it. If Danaë within a brazen tower had never been immured, Jupiter would ne'er have made her great with child. Juno, by setting strict watch on Io with her horned brow, made her, in Jupiter's regard, more precious than before.

He who desires the safe and easy way, let him go pluck the leaves of the trees and drink of the open river. Ah, my dears, if you would keep your hold upon your lovers, learn to misuse them oft. Alas! And must I give you lessons to my own undoing. It matters not. Let him who will, love the pattern woman who will always do as she's told; I can't abide her. I flee who chases me, and chase who flees me.

Now, you, good sir, who think your wife so very safe; from this day forth bolt up your door at night-fall; ask who it is that comes so often and taps so cautiously; what makes your dogs bark at the dead of night; what notes are those with which that servant girl so slyly comes and goes; ask why your fair one wants so often to have her bed to herself. Let these gnawing fears at length invade the marrow of your bones, and thus compel me to use some stratagem.

He's only fit to pilfer the sand of the lonely shore who can love the wife of a complacent fool. I give you solemn warning, if you don't keep watch upon your wife, she soon will cease to be my mistress. I have been a long-suffering individual. I hoped the day would come when your jealous watch would put me on my mettle. But you don't bestir yourself at all. You bear what never husband in the world should bear. Well, 'tis I myself will put an end to this too facile love.

Oh, luckless that I am! Will you never shut your door against me? Shall I never have, o' nights, to risk your vengeance? Shall I never have anything to fear from you? Will never the gasping intake of the breath disturb my sleep? You'll ne'er do aught would make me wish you dead. Do I, of all men, want an easy-going husband, a husband who would prostitute his wife? You poison my pleasure by your feeble acquiescence. Why don't you look for some one to whom such meekness would be welcome? If you wish that I should be your rival, then swear your rival I shall never be.

THE LOVES

BOOK III

ELEGY I

THE TRAGIC AND THE ELEGIAC MUSE STRIVE FOR THE POSSESSION OF OVID

THERE is an age-old forest which for many a year the ax has never touched. They say that it is sacred to a god. In its midst is a sacred well sheltered by a grotto, hewn out of the rock; and all around, birds sing their sweet complaint. One day, as I was sauntering in its shady groves, I fell to wondering what task should occupy my Muse.

And making her way towards me I beheld Elegy. All perfumed was her hair and right cunningly braided, and, if I saw aright, one of her feet was longer than the other. Her mien was staid, her form was comely; her dress of thinnest gauze, and, in her eyes, the light of love, and even her maimèd foot lent her an added charm. And Tragedy also I beheld, advancing with measured strides and vehement gesture, her hair disheveled, her mantle sweeping the ground. In her left hand she proudly bore the royal scepter, and on her feet she wore the Lydian buskin.

First of the twain she spake to me and said, "When wilt thou have finished with thy loves, O poet, heedless of thy great calling? At drunken revels they talk of thy wild doings, and at the crossways, too, thou art a byword. Often, as you pass by, men point you out and say, 'There goes the man whom cruel Love consumes.' Knowest thou not thou art the talk of the whole town, thou who with shameless tongue vauntest thy exploits in the lists of love? High time it is to essay a higher theme. Long enough hast thou been idle; take up a loftier argument. The subject-matter of thy songs hampers thy genius; sing the noble deeds of war. 'This,' wilt thou say, 'is the field that befits my genius.' The songs the fair may sing, thy Muse has gayly told, and to such wanton trifles thy early youth didst thou devote. But now to me thy genius consecrate, so unto thee my name of Roman Tragedy I may owe. Thy genius is equal to this lofty task." She spake, and leaning proudly on her broidered buskins, thrice, nay four times, she shook her head, shadowed with cloudy hair.

Elegy, if my memory serves me, gave me a sidelong glance and smiled. She had—or do I dream?—a branch of myrtle in her hand. "Why, haughty Queen," she said, "dost thou rebuke me with such weighty words? Canst thou never lay aside thine austere air? For the nonce, at least, thou hast deigned to combat me in verses of unequal length, and with the measure that belongs to me. Not that I dare compare thy stately verse with mine; thy lofty palace quite o'er-whelms my lowly dwelling. Light as the air am I, and just as light is Cupid with whom I love to sport. I'm just as airy as the subject-matter of my song. Were it not for me, even Cupid's mother would lack something of her charm. I am the helpmeet and confederate of that goddess. The door that would never open for thy buskin, swings wide at the gentle accents of my voice; still, if in this respect my power is mightier than thine, I owe it to the patience with which I suffer many things which thou wouldst be too haughty to endure. It was from me that Corinna learned to hoodwink her guard, to force the lock of a well-fastened door, to steal quietly from her bed clad in a short chemise and to find her way noiselessly in the darkness of night.

"How often have I beheld myself hung on an unfriendly door, caring not a whit whether I was read by the passers-by. Nay more; I remember that Corinna's maid received me and kept me hidden in her bosom till her mistress's grim guardian had turned his back on us. Shall I remind thee how, to celebrate thy fair one's birthday, thou didst send me to her as a present, and how she tore me into fragments and cast me pitilessly into the water? 'Twas I who first made stir within thee the fertile seeds of poetry; to me thou owest the happy talent which my rival would claim for herself."

At length the Muses both were silent, and in these words I addressed them: "By your own selves," I said, "I conjure you. With friendly ears, I pray, list to my faltering words. Thou offerest me, thou, the scepter and the stately buskin, and even now from contact with thy lips, accents sublime have issued from my mouth; whilst thou, even thou, upon my loves bestowest immortality. Hear then my prayers and suffer me to wed the greater with the lesser verse; grant me, proud Tragedy, a little respite. Thy service needeth years, thy rival's, merely hours. She was not deaf to my regrets; now may the tender loves make haste to profit by the time thus granted me; for, in my rear, a far more weighty task is pressing on."

ELEGY II

THE CIRCUS

THOUGH I am sitting here, it's not in the least because I am interested in the racing; all the same I want your favorite to win. What I've come here for is to talk to you, to sit near you and to tell you how tremendously I love you. So you are looking at the races, I am looking at you. Let us both enjoy the sight that pleases, both drink our fill of delight. He's a lucky fellow, the man you back; he has the good fortune to enlist your interest. I wish I had his chance; like a flash I should be at the starting-post, and let my horses run clean away with me. Here, I'd shake the reins about their necks, here, I'd let them feel the whip, then round I'd go within a hair's breadth of the turning-post. But if, in my headlong career, I chanced to catch sight of you, I should pull up and the reins would drop from my hands. Ah, how narrowly Pelops escaped falling by a spear at Pisa, through gazing on thy face, Hippodamia! Nevertheless, he won because his mistress favored him. May all lovers thus triumph when their ladies want them to.

Why do you keep trying to edge away from me? You can't do it; we've got to sit close because of the seats. That's an advantage I owe to the Circus arrangements. But you, there, who are sitting on the other side of this lady, mind what you're about; don't lean on her like that. And you behind there; don't thrust out your legs like that; don't let your hard knee dig into her back. Mind, darling, you're letting your dress drag on the ground. Pull it up a little, or I shall have to do it for you. Ah, jealous dress, how you liked to cover her beautiful legs. Aye, and the longer you looked —oh, you jealous dress, you! Atalanta's legs must have looked like yours, when she was running—no wonder Milanion wanted to catch hold of them—and Diana's too, when, with uplifted dress, she pursueth the wild beasts in the forests, beasts less fearless than herself. Though I never saw them, those legs set me on fire. What would happen if I saw yours? You will be adding fuel to fire, water to the ocean. I can just imagine, from what I've seen, what those other charms are like that you conceal so well under your dainty dress.

Would you like to have a little cool air in your face? If I wave this tablet a little it will refresh you, unless it's the warmth of my passion rather than the warmth of the air that is heating you, and lighting up such a charming flame in your heart. While I've been speaking, a horrid black smut has come and settled on your white dress. Begone, base smudge, from those snowy shoulders. But here they come; keep still and drink it all in. Now's the time to clap; the procession is coming in all its splendor.

First of all comes Victory, with wings outspread. Be kind to me, O goddess, and help my love to win. Three cheers for Neptune, you rash people that put your trust in the sea. As for me, I don't like it. I prefer my own bit of land. You, my soldier friend, shout loud for Mars, he is your god. I loathe fighting. I love peace and love that thrives with peace. Let Phœbus be propitious to the augurs, and Phœbe to the huntsmen, and you, Minerva, receive the salutations of the craftsmen. And you, ye tillers of the soil, give hail to Ceres and to kindly Bacchus. May Pollux hearken to the gladiators' prayers and Castor to the horseman's. For us, 'tis thee, sweet Venus, thee and the Loves, thy bowmen, that we greet with cheers. Oh, help me, tender goddess; change thou my fair one's heart, that she may let herself be loved. See, Venus nods, and seems to tell me I shall win. What she foretells, tell me yourself, I pray. Hear thou my prayer and—Venus forgive me—you will be greater than that goddess herself. I swear it, and all the gods that shine in that procession I call to witness, you shall ever be my darling mistress. But you've nowhere to rest your legs. Put your toes, if you like, on these bars. They've cleared the course now, and the big races are going to begin. The prætor's just given the signal. The four-horsed chariots are off. I see your favorite. Whoever you favor is bound to win. The very horses seem to guess your wishes. Ye gods, how wide he takes them round the turning-post. Wretched creature, what are you about? Now you've let your rival get ahead of you. He went round ever so much more closely. What *are* you up to, foolish one? What's the use of a woman's backing you. For heaven's sake pull your left rein hard.

Oh, he's an idiot, our man. Come on, Romans, have him back, wave your togas there. See they're calling him back. But mind they don't ruffle your hair, waving their togas about like that; come and hide your head in the folds of mine.

Look, now they're starting again, the bars are down. Here they come, with their different colors, driving like mad. Beat them this time, anyhow; you've got a clear field in front of you. See that my mistress has her way, and see that I have mine. Well, she's got hers; but I must wait. He's won. Now I must see what I can do. She smiled, the darling, and there was a promise in her look. That's enough for here. Elsewhere you'll let me have the rest.

ELEGY III

TO HIS MISTRESS, WHOM HE HAS FOUND TO BE FORSWORN

SHALL I believe any longer that the gods exist? She has broken her sworn oath, and her loveliness is unimpaired. Long was her hair before she took the gods to witness. Now that she has deceived them, it is just as long. The whiteness of her skin was suffused with the hue of the rose, and the rose still blooms on her snowy cheek. She had a little foot; her foot is still the daintiest thing on earth. Tall was she, and graceful. Tall and graceful is she still. Her eyes shone like stars; many a time with them has she deceived me.

And so the gods themselves allow beautiful women to break their vow, and Beauty herself is a goddess. It was, I remember, only the other day that she swore by her own eyes and by mine; it was mine that felt the smart. Ye gods, if the deceitful little thing has hoodwinked you, how is it you have punished me for her crime? It is true you did not hesitate to decree death to the daughter of Cepheus, in punishment for her mother's pride. If I have found you vain and ineffectual witnesses, if she plumes herself on having fooled us both, have I got to suffer for her perjury, have I to be at once her scapegoat and her dupe?

Either the gods exist in name alone, a mere chimæra invented to terrify the silly credulous rabble, or, if exist they do, they display gross favoritism towards women, and let them do what they like. It is only against us men that Mars is armed with his death-dealing sword; only against us that Pallas turns her fatal spear. At us Apollo aims his arrows. At us, and us alone, the thunderbolt is sped from sovran Jove's right hand. The gods have not the courage to punish the misdeeds of women, and not being able to terrify them, are themselves in terror of them. And are we going on burning incense on their altars? No, men ought to have more spirit.

Jupiter demolishes sacred woods and citadels, but he withholds his wrath from perjured women. Out of the whole host of lying jades, only Semele perished by the flames. And that was because she was so willing. If she had evaded the attentions of her lover, the father of Bacchus would never have had to do a mother's duties.

And why do I thus fall out with all the company of heaven? The gods have eyes, as we have, they have hearts like ours. If I were a god myself, I should never quarrel with a woman because she took my name in vain. I should swear that the jade swore truly, and I'd never be known for a crusty god.

But you, my dear, use the gods a little more sparingly; or at all events have a thought for your lover's eyes.

ELEGY IV

HE URGES A HUSBAND NOT TO KEEP SO STRICT A
WATCH ON HIS WIFE

IMPOSSIBLE man, you have set some one to watch the doings of your young wife. It is quite useless. A woman's
only armor is her virtue. She alone is chaste who is not kept
chaste by fear. She who sins not because she must not, sins
just the same. You may keep her body intact, but she's
a rake at heart. You can't keep watch upon a woman's
thoughts. Nor, indeed, though you bolt and bar every door,
can you safeguard her body. Though you think to keep the
whole world out, there'll be a traitor within. Whoso is
free to err, to err is less inclined. The very power to sin
weakens the seed of vice. Do not, I pray you, prick on her
desire by putting restraints upon her. Be easy with her and
you'll gain your end more readily.

It was only the other day I saw a horse, impatient of the
curb, rushing along with the speed of lightning; and then, no
sooner did he feel the reins lying loose upon his neck, than
he calmly came to a standstill. We are always eager for forbidden things, and yearn for what is denied us, like the sick
man who longs for water because his doctor forbids him to
drink it.

A hundred eyes had Argus in his forehead, a hundred eyes
behind, but Love was often one too many for him. Danaë
was immured a virgin in her eternal chamber of rock and
bronze, yet Danaë became a mother. Penelope, though there
was none to guard her, remained undefiled among a host of
young and lusty suitors.

The more carefully a thing is guarded, the more we long
for it. All this watchfulness and fuss is merely inviting the

attentions of the robber. Few people want the pleasures they are free to take. It's not your wife's good looks, it's the fuss you make of her that makes men want your wife. They think she must be wonderful indeed thus to have captivated you. She may be a faithless baggage, the woman whom her husband guards so jealously; she may be a strumpet; she's, all the same, a treasure. The risks one runs in order to possess her count even more than the object possessed. A fig for your indignation! I tell you, I only love forbidden pleasures. The only woman I care to have is the one that says, "I'm terrified." Moreover, you've no right to treat a free-born woman like a slave. You should only use foreign importations so. Doubtless you want her keeper to say, "I kept her chaste." You want your slave, I suppose, to get all the credit.

A man must really be a bumpkin who takes his wife's unfaithfulness to heart. He can't know much about the morals of the Capital. Why Ilia, who bore both Romulus and Remus after her affair with Mars, was not exactly a paragon of virtue. Why go and marry a pretty woman, if you want a virtuous wife? Good looks and virtue don't go hand in hand.

If you're a wise man, you'll give her a little more rope; you'll look a bit more amiable and not be always playing the stern husband and preaching about your rights. And cultivate the friends your wife will bring you; there will be no lack of them. You'll thus get the maximum of credit with the minimum of cost. Thus you'll always have plenty of gay young sparks around you and see about the house all manner of nice things you never had to pay for.

ELEGY V

A DREAM

'TWAS night, and sleep had weighed down my weary eyelids, when this vision came to terrify my soul.

On the side of a hill looking towards the south was a grove thickly planted with oaks, and multitudes of birds found shelter amid their branches. Beneath was a wide expanse clad in freshest green, watered by a stream which flowed on with a sweet murmur.

Beneath the shade of a leafy oak I was endeavoring to avoid the heat, but it was hot even in the tree's shade. And lo, grazing on the jeweled meadow, a white heifer came in sight, a heifer whiter than fresh-fallen snow ere it has melted into clear water; whiter than the foam on the milk of the ewe that has just been milked.

Near her was a bull, her happy mate. He lay down beside her on the thick green carpet; and as he lay thus at his ease, he slowly chewed the cud of tender grass. Soon, sleep robbing him of his strength, methought he lay his hornèd head upon the ground for very weariness.

Hither came a crow swiftly cleaving the air and, croaking hoarsely, lighted upon the green sward. Thrice did she plunge her ravening beak into the breast of the snow-white heifer, and then at length she flew away. But a black stain was on the breast of the heifer. And when she saw afar off bulls browsing on the pastures (for afar off other bulls were browsing on the pastures) she rushed away and mingled with them and sought out a spot where the soil was more fertile.

"Come," I cried, "come, interpreter of dreams, and tell me what, if indeed it hath a meaning, this dream of mine betokens." Then did the interpreter of the dreams of night

ponder upon my dream, and thus at length he made reply.
"The heat which thou wast fain to escape in the leafy shade,
and which thou couldst not avoid, was the heat of love. The
heifer is thy mistress, for of such whiteness is she. Thou
thyself art the bull which was following his mate. The crow
whose sharp beak tore at the heifer's breast was that old
procuress who will corrupt thy loved one. The long hesi-
tation of the heifer and her final abandonment of the bull
means that thou wilt be left cold on thy solitary couch.
The wound and the dark stains beneath her breast show that
she is not free from the soilure of adultery."

Thus spake the reader of dreams; my cheeks were white
and cold and the drear night spread out before mine eyes.

ELEGY VI

TO A RIVER WHICH HAS OVERFLOWED ITS BANKS AND
HINDERED THE POET, WHO WAS HASTENING TO
HIS MISTRESS

RIVER, whose soft, muddy banks are overgrown with
reeds, I am hastening to my mistress. Stay thy course
a while. No bridge hast thou, nor oarless bark to ferry me
with a rope across thy stream.

But lately thou wast just a rivulet, I mind me well, and
fearlessly I traversed thee on foot, and in thy deepest part
thou scarce did wet my ankles. Now, swollen by the melting snows from yonder mountain, thou rushest wildly on and
along thy muddy course pourest a foaming mass of waters.

What did it boot me so to press my speed, to have snatched
such scanty rest, to have turned night into day, if here I
needs must halt, if to the farther bank I have no means to
cross? Oh, wherefore do I lack the wings which bore the

heroic son of Danaë when he carried off Medusa's head swarming with dreadful serpents? Now long I for the chariot whence came the seed of Ceres, scattered o'er the stubborn soil. Alas these wonders, save in a poet's dream, were never wrought. Never were they seen of man, and never man will see them. But thou, O stream that overflowest thy wide banks, flow on within thy bounds, and so flow on for ever. Ne'er couldst thou bear the weight of public shame, if it were known thou stayedst a lover's steps.

Verily rivers should help an eager lover on his way, for rivers themselves have known the pangs of love. Pale Inachus, they say, was smitten with the charms of Melie, the Bithynian nymph, and his chill waters warmed with his love for her. Troy had not borne its ten long years of siege, O Xanthus, when Neæra drew thy gaze. What made Alpheus wander through so many lands if not his passion for a maid of Arcady? And thou, Peneus, when Creusa unto Xanthus was betrothed, hid her, so 'tis held, within the land of the Phthiotians.

Why should I tell of Asopus, whom warlike Thebe took to her bosom, Thebe fated to give five daughters to the world? And thou, O Acheloüs, if I ask of thee to-day, "Where are thy horns?" thou wouldst with sorrow make reply and say that in his wrath Hercules did break them off. What Hercules would not have done for Calydon, would not have done for all Ætolia, he did for Dejanira and for her alone. The Nile itself, the mighty river that through seven mouths flows to the sea and hides so well the secret of its source, could not with all its waters overwhelm the flame with which he burned for Evadne, Asopus' daughter. Enipeus, so he might embrace the daughter of Salmoneus, commanded his waters to recede, and, obedient to his command, those waters did recede. Nor thee will I forget who, flowing down thy rocky bed, waterest with thy foam-

ing stream the fruitful fields of Argive Tibur; nor thee whom
Ilia charmed, albeit in sorry plight was she, her hair, her
features torn with her own nails, mourning her uncle's sacrilegious crimes, and the outrage wrought by Mars, wandering bare-footed in solitary places. Her, from his swift-flow-
ing waters, the generous river saw, and raising his head above
the flood called hoarsely to her, saying, "Wherefore in sorrow
wanderest thou by my banks, O Ilia, seed of Laomedon of
Ida? Whither hath thy raiment gone? Whither bendest
thou thy lonely steps? Wherefore doth the white fillet bind
not thy rangèd hair? Wherefore dost thou weep and mar
thy brimming eyes with tears? Why thus in frenzy beat
thy naked breast? A heart of stone or brass that man must
have, who on a lovely face all stained with tears can look
unmoved by pity. Ilia, fear no more; for thee my palace
will fling wide its portals, my waters from all harm shall keep
thee. Ilia, fear no more; over a hundred nymphs or more
thou shalt be queen, for a hundred nymphs or more beneath
my waters dwell. Oh, spurn me not, I pray, thou seed of
Troy; gifts richer than my promises thou shalt have."

He spake; and Ilia, with downcast eyes, bathed with tears
her heaving bosom. Thrice she essayed to fly; thrice she
stayed her steps by the edge of the deep waters, for fear
would not suffer her to flee. Howbeit, at last, tearing her
hair with hostile hand, with trembling lips thus sorrowfully
she spake: "O would to heaven my bones had been gathered
up and laid in the tomb of my fathers while yet I was a
virgin. Wherefore to marriage dost thou invite me, a vestal
yesterday, to-day unworthy to tend the sacred fire of Ilium?
Why should I longer tarry? E'en now they point at me
with scornful finger and exclaim, 'Behold the adulteress.'
Let me die, and with me die the shame that suffers me not
to raise my eyes without a blush." She said, and veiling
with her robe her lovely weeping eyes, she cast herself de-

spairingly into the swirling flood. The River, so 'tis said, upstayed her, placing his hand beneath her breast, and took her as a bride to the bridal bed.

And thou, like enough, hast burned with love for a maiden; but thou hast woods and forests to hide thy little failings. Even as I speak, thy waters swell still more, and thy bed, broad though it be, is not wide enough to hold the tributary streams that flow to thee from every side. What grievance hast thou against me, thou angry river; why dost thou delay the pleasures of a pair of lovers; why hold me up so roughly on my way? If only thou didst flow with waters of thine own, if only thou wert a river with a name, if thy fame throughout the world were known! But name hast thou none; thy waters come from little tributary brooks; thy source and even thy course are uncertain. Thy spring is the rain and melted snow, and these thou owest to sluggish winter. Either in winter-tide thou rollest thy turgid waters, or else, in summer, thy bed is but a dry and sandy track. What traveler then has e'er found water enough to quench his thirst and say to thee in thankfulness of heart, "Flow on, flow on for ever!"

Onward thou flowest, harmful to flocks and herds, more harmful still to crops. For these things let others grieve, my own ills suffice for me. Fool that I am, this stream I told how rivers love. It shames me to have spoken of names so great before so miserable a brook. What was I dreaming of, to speak to it of Acheloüs and of Inachus, and of thee, wide-flowing Nile?

Out on thee, muddy torrent. Scorching summers and rainless winters ever be thy lot!

ELEGY VII

THE POET REPROACHES HIMSELF FOR HAVING FAILED IN HIS DUTY TOWARDS HIS MISTRESS

IS she not fair, is she not accomplished? Have I not long hungered to possess her? Yet she, yes, she of all women in the world, I have held in my arms and to no purpose. To my shame I confess it, I have lain like a lifeless hulk upon her couch, strengthless and still. Despite my longings, despite my loved one's longings, I could not stir myself into life. In vain about my neck she twined her ivory arms, dear arms, more white than Thracian snows. In vain her tongue she thrust and thrust against my tongue, and slipped her amorous thigh beneath my own; vainly she lavished on me all her sweetest names, called me her conqueror and said the things that women are wont to say in such a pass; it was as though my members had been rubbed with chilling hemlock and knew no more the way to do their duty. Like to a trunk I lay, like to a lifeless statue, a useless mass, so that indeed she might have doubted whether I were in sooth a man, or but the simulacrum of a man.

What shall I do when I am old, supposing that I live so long, if I fail so lamentably now that I am young? Alas, I blush for my youth. I am young, I am a man, and I could not prove to my mistress that I was either. She left her bed, even as the holy priestess that watches the everlasting flame of Vesta, or as a chaste sister saying farewell to a beloved brother. Howbeit, it was but lately that I paid my debt twice over with the fair-haired Chloe; thrice with the white-skinned Pitho; thrice again with Libas; and, by Corinna urged, nine times in one short night I fought with honor in the lists of love.

Was it some magic philter that benumbed my limbs to-day? Was it some incantation, or some poisonous herb that put me in such a sorry plight? Was it some witch that wrote my name on the crimson wax and plunged a needle into my liver? The corn, stricken by a witch's curse, soon dwindles into sterile grass, the springs run dry, the acorn falls from the oak, the grape from the vine and the fruit drops from the tree, though no one shake the bough. Since this is so, why should not magic numb the nerves? Perchance 'twas magic that turned me into ice. And then, think on the shame of the thing! Yes, my very shame robbed me of my strength. Shame was the secondary cause of my undoing.

How fair, withal, was she on whom I was free to look, and whom I was free to touch, for I touched her, even as the shift she wore. At that sweet contact the King of Pylos would have grown young again, Tithonus would have felt strange promptings for his years. In her I found a woman; she found not in me a man. To what fresh vows, to what new prayer shall I have recourse to-day? Doubtless the gods regret they ever gave me such a prize, seeing the shameful use I made of it.

I longed with feverish longing to be admitted to her house; I was admitted; to kiss her, and I kissed her; to lie with her, I lay with her. What availed me my good fortune? To be a king and wield no scepter? Like a miser in the midst of wealth, I owned my riches, but I could not use them. Thus was the prying Tantalus consumed with thirst, with water all around; thus saw he fruit on which he ne'er could lay his hand; thus in the morning, the husband leaves his wife in order to go stainless to the altar of the gods.

Maybe, you'll say, she did not shower on me kisses most passionate and most sweet; she did not do her utmost to excite me. The stoutest oaks, the hardest adamant, the sternest rocks would have been moved by her caresses. She would have moved any living thing, anything you could dub a man. But then, alas, I was neither living nor a man. What pleasure would the songs of Phemius bring to ears that could not hear? What pleasure would a picture give to sightless Thamyris?

What delights, withal, I had secretly promised myself, what different ways of enjoying her had I imagined. And yet my body, shame on it, was like a dead thing, more drooping than a rose of yesterday. And look at it now, and high time it is, see how it is coming back to life again; see how it is asking to be up and doing, to get to work once more. Why are you not overcome with shame, thou vilest part of me? That was how you made a fool of me before, promising what you did not fulfill. Through you my mistress was deceived, through you I found myself a defaulter, through you I suffered the most painful affront, the most grievous damage.

And yet my mistress disdains not to incite me with her dainty hand. But seeing that all her arts were vain, that my body, forgetful of its former prowess, would give no sign of life, cried, "Why do you play the fool with me? Who asked you, madman that you are, to come to bed with me against your will? Or has some enchantress of Æxa, with her needle and her wool, bewitched you? Or have you been spending your strength on some other woman?"

So saying, she leapt from the bed with nothing on but her flimsy shift, and fled away bare-footed. And, as she would not have her servants know she had come unscathed from the combat, she went and laved herself with water to dissemble the affront.

ELEGY VIII

TO HIS MISTRESS, COMPLAINING THAT SHE HAS GIVEN PREFERENCE TO A WEALTHIER RIVAL

AND who now attaches any value to the liberal arts, or looks on poetry as worth a straw? Time was when genius was held more precious than gold; now, if you've no money, you are accounted the veriest barbarian. My books have the good fortune to please my mistress. They have the entrée to her; I, alas, have not. She has given high praise to the poetry, but on the poet she has shut her door. I am told that I'm a genius, yet they leave me to cool my heels where I can. Any rich parvenu who has swash-bucklered his way to wealth is set above me.

Can you, my life, really be so scatter-brained as to put your arms about him? Can you, my life, let him put his arms about you? Let me tell you, in case you know it not, that that head of his was recently covered by a helmet, and that a sword hung from that side which now is so devoted to you. His left hand, with the gold ring which fits it so ill, bore a shield; touch his right hand, and you'll find it bathed with blood. The man's a murderer! Can you really hold his hand? What has become of that soft heart of yours? Count those scars, the records of the fights that he's been through. All that he has, he won at the price of his blood. Perhaps he will tell you how many throats he has cut. And are you so greedy for money that you can touch such cruel hands, while I, innocent priest of Apollo and the Muses, vainly lay my verses at your unheeding door?

You, who are wise, learn not our useless poet's lore; learn rather to march with noisy troops and to follow the career of war. Instead of trying to be a poet, learn to be a soldier.

Even if you were Homer himself, only thus could you obtain the favors of the fair. Jupiter knew well enough that nothing is so powerful as gold, and he won the virgin on whom he had cast his eye by changing himself to gold. So long as gold was not forthcoming he found himself face to face with an obdurate father, an inflexible damsel, doors of brass and a tower of iron; but no sooner did the would-be seducer arrive with presents than she unveiled her bosom, and forthwith gave—what she was asked to give.

It was not thus in aged Saturn's reign. Then all the metals were buried deep within the bowels of the earth. Bronze and silver, gold and heavy iron to the shades he had committed. In those olden days no treasure heaps were seen. But better things earth gave than that, rich harvests from the unlaborious earth, fruits in abundance and stores of honey laid in the hollow oak. None ever broke the soil with the patient plow, no land surveyor parceled out the soil; no oars smote the tossing waves. For mortals, then, the shores of the sea were barriers impassable. Against thyself, O Man, hast thou turned thy powers of invention, and used thy genius to invent evils untold. What hath it availed thee to girdle your cities round with towers and ramparts, and among men to stir up armed war? What is the sea to thee? The earth might have sufficed thee. There is another realm to conquer—the sky; wherefore attack it not? To the heavens, too, thou dost aspire, so far as thou mayest. Quirinus, Bacchus, Alcides, and, now, Cæsar have each their temple.

We dig the earth for gold instead of golden harvests. The soldier possesses wealth obtained by blood. The Senate shuts its doors against the poor; money paves the way to honors. Money makes the solemn judge, the haughty knight. Let them have everything; let them lord it over the Campus Martius and the Forum; let them decide on peace or war; but in their greediness let them draw the line at robbing me of my mistress, and I shall be content. They must leave something to the poor man.

But nowadays, any woman, be she as prudish as the Sabines, is treated like a chattel-slave by any man who can throw about his money. Now, I'm always stopped by this keeper fellow, and she says that she's in mortal terror of her husband. If I could afford costly presents, both of them would disappear as by magic. Oh, if there be a god who will avenge the unrequited lover, let him reduce such ill-gotten wealth to dust.

ELEGY IX

ON THE DEATH OF TIBULLUS

IF the mother of Memnon, if the mother of Achilles, mourned for their dead sons; if the mighty goddesses are not insensible to the blows of Fate, then, plaintive Elegy, unbind thy sorrowing tresses; never, alas, did thy name so well befit thee as at this hour. Tibullus, whom thou didst inspire, Tibullus thy glory, is but a lifeless corse that the flames of the pyre will soon consume. See how Venus' son goes with his quiver reversed, with broken bow and extinguished torch. Look you how sadly he fares, with drooping wings; and how with cruel hand he strikes his naked breast. The tear-drops fall amid his floating hair; his mouth gives forth the sound of broken sobs. So from thy palace went he forth, gracious Iulus, to mourn for the death of Æneas, his brother. Venus herself grieved no less for the death of Tibullus, than for the death of her young lover, whose groin was pierced by a wild boar, before her eyes.

And yet we poets are called sacred, the favorites of the gods. And some there are who behold in us a hint of the divine. Nevertheless, inexorable death profanes all hallowed things, and lays on all that lives his unseen hand. What could his mother, what could his father do, for Ismarian Orpheus? What did it avail him that he had tamed and softened with his song the creatures of the wilds?   Linus came of the same father, and Apollo is said to have mourned him in the deep forest on his reluctant lyre.   Then there is the Mæonian bard, the unfailing spring where the poets ever draw nigh to drink the Pierian spring.   For him also came the day of death, the day that hurled him to the depths of dark Avernus.   'Tis poetry alone that 'scapes the all-consuming pyre.   The work of the poet knows not death; the story of Troy's siege and all its toils and the unfinished web will ever be remembered. So Nemesis and Delia shall have a lasting name, the one his last, the other his first love.

What now can sacrifices offered to the gods avail thee? What can the sistra of Egypt do for thee now?   What boots it to lie apart in a lonely bed?   When I see how even the most virtuous are snatched away by cruel fate, forgive me when I say I am tempted to believe that the gods do not exist.   Live a holy life; despite your sanctity, you will surely die.   Pay service to the gods; for all your piety, death will tear you from the temple and hurry you into the grave. Think you your poetry will save you?   See how Tibullus lies low.   With all that remains of so great a poet, you scarce could fill a tiny urn.

What, is it thou, O sacred poet, that the flames of the pyre have just consumed?   They had not feared to feast upon thy vitals.   They might have devoured the gilded temples of the mightiest of the gods, seeing that to thee they were so cruel. Venus turned away her head, and some aver that she could not restrain her tears.

Yet was the poet's lot less lamentable than if he had died among the Phæacians and had been buried unhonored and unknown.   Here at least a mother closed his misty eyes, and paid him the last sad rites. Here at least a sister shared her unhappy mother's grief, and with disheveled locks came to sorrow over his grave. Nemesis and Delia both printed on thy lips a final kiss and quitted not thy pyre. Delia, as at length she turned away, said, " 'Tis I was made the happier by your love; thou didst live while yet I was the object of your flame!" "What is that thou sayest?" said Nemesis. "What need for thee to bewail my loss? 'Twas me, as he lay dying, he clasped with his failing hand."

Still if aught remains of us but a name and a shadow, Tibullus will live on in the valleys of Elysium. Come forth to meet him, learned Catullus, come with thy Calvus, and wreathe thy youthful brow with ivy. And Gallus, come thou too (if they wrong thee who say thou wrongedst a friend), prodigal of thy blood and of thy life. Of these thy shade is the companion, and if a shade be aught, thou hast swelled the blessed throng, gracious Tibullus. Rest ye, his bones, at peace within the quiet urn, and may the earth lie lightly on his ashes.

ELEGY X

HE COMPLAINS TO CERES THAT, DURING HER FESTIVAL, HE IS NOT SUFFERED TO SHARE HIS MISTRESS' COUCH

HERE is the yearly festival of Ceres come round again: and my lady has to sleep in a lonely bed. Golden-tressèd Ceres, with thy fine hair adorned with ears of corn, wherefore, on thy feast day, dost thou deny us our pleasure? All the world over, the nations laud thy generosity and no other divinity looks upon us mortals with more favoring eye.

In the earliest times the rude inhabitants of the countryside never baked their bread, and the threshing floor was for them a name unknown. But upon the oaks, the earliest oracles, grew acorns; these and the tender shoots of grass were the food of man. It was Ceres who first taught him how to plant the seed in the earth so that it should swell and, with the sickle, to reap the golden corn; she it was who first compelled the bulls to bear the yoke and clove, with the plow's sharp tooth, the ground that too long had been lying fallow. Can any one believe that she delights in the tears of lovers, and that the way to her favor is to lie in lonely misery? Nay, though she takes pleasure in the labor of the fields, she is not coy and awkward, nor is her heart impervious to love. I call the Cretans to witness, and 'tis not all fable that you hear in Crete, so proud of having nurtured mighty Jove. There was reared the Sovereign of the starry realms; 'twas there that with his baby lips he sucked the sweet milk. Here the witnesses are worthy of credence; their foster-child will vouch for the truth of what they tell and Ceres, I think, will confess to a frailty of which the whole world knows.

At the foot of Mount Ida the goddess had perceived the youthful Iasius, who, with unerring aim, was slaying the wild beasts. She saw, and suddenly she felt her marrow on fire with a secret flame. On one side shame, on the other love, were striving to possess her heart. Love triumphed over shame. Thenceforth you might have seen the furrows grow dry, and the earth produced scarcely as many grains of corn as had been sown. When, with the mattock, he had thoroughly turned over the soil and with the plow had broken the stubborn glebe, when he had scattered the seed evenly over his wide fields, the hopes of the husbandman were brought to nought.

The goddess who watches over the crops was dallying in the deep forests. The wreaths of corn had fallen from her long tresses. Only in Crete was the year fruitful and the harvests abundant. Wheresoever the goddess had passed, the earth was thick with crops. Ida, so rich in trees, grew white with corn and the wild boar cropped the corn in the woodlands. Minos, the lawgiver, wished for many such years and longed for the love of Ceres to endure.

The pain thou wouldst have endured, O fair-tressed goddess, if thou hadst been compelled to sleep away from thy lover, I am forced to undergo on this day that is hallowed to thy mysteries. Wherefore must I be sad, when thou hast found again a daughter, a queen only less exalted than Juno herself? Such a holiday invites to Love, to Song and to Wine. Such are the offerings it behoves us to make to the gods that rule the world.

ELEGY XI

WEARY AT LENGH OF HIS MISTRESS' INFIDELITIES, HE SWEARS THAT HE WILL LOVE HER NO LONGER

I HAVE had a lot to put up with, and I've put up with it a great deal too long. I am completely out of patience with you. My heart is tired out. Away with you, base Love! My slavery is over; I have escaped my fetters, and what I bore without shame, it now shames me to have borne at all. I've won the day; Love is vanquished. I trample it beneath my feet. True, I've been a long time plucking up courage. Fight on, my soul, and faint not. It is a wrench, indeed, but some day you'll be glad you bore this present pain. A bitter potion has oftentimes brought succor to the sick.

How could I have sunk so low, after so many rebuffs, as to lie down on the hard ground outside your door? Could

I for some other lover you had with you there, act the slave
and play the watchman outside the door that was shut against
me? I have seen him coming away from your house, looking a very worn-out warrior indeed. Seeing him was not
so bad as being seen by him, all the same. May such a disgrace befall my enemies. Tell me when I have ever failed
to be at your side, your escort, your lover, and your friend.
You owe your popularity to going about with me. It's because I loved you that you got so many lovers. What's the
use of my telling you about your lying tongue, and all the
solemn oaths you've broken to deceive me? What's the good
of referring to the ogling and winking that went on at dinner
between you and your young admirers, and the code words
employed to conceal the true sense of what you were saying.
One day they told me she was ill. I nearly had a fit, and
off I rushed. I get there and find—well, that she isn't too
ill to entertain my rival.

There! there are plenty of other instances I could give,
but that's the sort of thing I've had to put up with. Look
and see if you can find another man who would stand what
I have stood. Already I can hear the water rippling behind
my vessel's stern, hung with the votive wreath. Farewell.
No, I don't want any more kisses; and it's no good talking
like that any more; it's waste of time; your words don't
move me now. I'm not the madman I used to be.—Yet oh,
this wavering heart of mine! How it is torn this way and
that, wrung simultaneously by love and hate; and love, I
think, is winning the day. I will hate, if I am able; if not,
I will love, but not willingly. The ox, too, loves not the
yoke. He hates it; but still he bears it. Even as I fly your
perfidy, your beauty draws me back. I hate the depravity
of your soul; I love your body. Thus I can live neither with
you nor without you, and I know not what I want myself.
I would that you were less fair or less wicked. Such love-

liness goes ill with such evil ways. Your conduct bids me
hate; your beauty bids me love. Hapless indeed am I; her
charms outweigh the evil deeds of their possessor.

Forgive me, I beseech you, by the laws of our mutual love;
forgive me by all the gods who lend themselves so often to
thy false oaths; by that face that seems to me a thing divine,
and by thine eyes which have made captives of mine. Whatever you may be, you ever will be mine. Thine it is to say
whether you would have me a willing or unwilling lover.
Ah, let us spread our sails and profit by the prospering gales,
that, though against my will, I shall yet be forced to love.

ELEGY XII

HE LAMENTS THAT HIS POEMS HAVE MADE HIS MIS-
TRESS TOO WELL KNOWN

WHAT day was that, ye birds of mournful plumage,
when ye sang things of evil presage to my love-affairs?
What star shall I suspect is moving counter to my fate, what
gods shall I complain are making war against me? The
woman who but now confessed herself my own, of whom
I was the first the only lover, to-day I fear I share with
many rivals.

Am I at fault, or is it my verses that have made her the
talk? 'Tis even so. My genius hath made of her a wanton.
And I deserve it. For why did I vaunt her beauty? If she
sells herself to-day, mine is the fault. I am the power that
hath made her please; 'tis I who have brought her lovers;
these hands have opened the door to them.

Whether verses are good for aught, I much misdoubt me;
they have always wrought me ill. 'Twas they excited envy
of my treasure.

Though of Thebes I might sing, and Troy and Cæsar's mighty deeds, Corinna alone could fire my genius. Would to heaven that the Muses had been unfavorable to my songs and that Phœbus had deserted me when my task was but begun. Yet since it is the custom to give ear to what the poets say, I should not have wished my verses to have had no weight.

'Tis we who sang of Scylla stealing from her father's head his treasured locks and hiding in her womb the raging dogs. 'Tis we who have given wings to the feet and serpents to the hair, our song gave victory to Abos' child and the wingèd horse. 'Tis we gave Tityos his mighty stature, and to Cerberus gave his triple mouths and his serpent-crownèd head. Enceladus we made hurling the spear with a thousand arms, and through us a youthful sorceress overcame heroes by her magic spells. We imprisoned the winds of Æolus in the wine-skins of the Ithacan king; we made the prying Tantalus go mad with thirst, with water all around him; Niobe we changed into a rock, and a young maiden into a bear. 'Tis thanks to us that the bird of Cecrops sings Odrysian Itys; that Jove transforms himself into a bird, or into gold, or, taking on the semblance of a bull, cleaves the waters with a maiden on his back. Why tell of Proteus and those dragon's teeth whence sprang the Thebans? Shall I tell of the bulls that spewed forth flames, and of the tears of amber that flowed, Orega, from thy sister's cheeks; of ships changed into sea goddesses; of the sun shrinking in horror from the sight of Atreus' dreadful feast and of the rocks that followed the music of the lyre?

Unceasing the genius of the poets pours forth, and recks not of the trammels of historic truth. Thus the praises of my mistress should have been looked upon as false. I have been undone by your credulity.

ELEGY XIII

THE FESTIVAL OF JUNO AT FALISCI

AS my wife was born at fruitful Falisci, we went to visit those walls which long ago were conquered, Camillus, by thee. The priestesses were making ready to celebrate the festival of the chaste Juno by holding solemn games and by the sacrifice of a heifer native to the place. It was a strong motive for lingering there awhile, to witness the rite, though full steep is the path that leads to the scene of its performance.

It is an immemorial grove, and so dense is the foliage there that the daylight cannot penetrate the gloom. One needs but to behold it, to realize that it is the abode of a divinity. An altar receives the prayers and incense offered by the faithful, a rough-hewn altar made by the artless folk of olden days. From this spot, once a year, as soon as the trumpet has given forth its solemn note, the procession sets out and makes its way along the carpeted paths. Snow-white heifers are led along amid the plaudits of the throng, heifers nourished by the grass of their native fields, and calves whose brows are not yet armed with threatening horns, and the humble pig, a lowlier victim, and the leader of the herd with horns curved back over his stubborn head. The goat alone is hateful to the lady goddess, ever since the day when by a goat her presence was betrayed in a deep wood and she was forced to abandon her flight. And so, even now, the boys pursue her with their darts and she is given as a prize to the one that brings her low.

All along the way the goddess is to pass, boys and shy maidens strew the paths with carpets. Gold and gems sparkle in their virgin hair and the proud mantle hides their gold-decked feet. In the Grecian manner of their ancestors they pass on, clad in white, and on their head they bear the sacred vessels entrusted to their care. Deep silence holds the people while the stately procession is passing by, and after her priestesses, follows the goddess herself.

The whole procession tells of Greece. After the murder of Agamemnon, Halesus fled the scene of his crime and the rich lands of his forefathers. It was only after many adventures, both by land and sea, that with auspicious hands he reared a high-walled city. 'Twas he that taught the Falisci to celebrate the rites of Juno. May they to me, and to her own people, ever be propitious.

ELEGY XIV

TO HIS MISTRESS

NAY, seeing how very beautiful you are, I won't deny you a few frailties. But what I don't want, and can't stand, is to know about them. No, I'm not going to take high moral ground; I'm not going to insist on your being a paragon of virtue and all that; but I want you to appear as if you were. A woman isn't guilty if she can deny the imputed delinquency. It's only confession that puts her out of court. How idiotic it is to prate every morning about what you did the night before, to proclaim in daylight what you did in the darkness.

Why, even a strumpet, before she attends to her customers, takes care to see that the street door is securely fastened. But you go blabbing about your misdeeds all over the place and seem to take a pride in putting yourself in the pillory. In future, if you can't be good, at least be cautious—assume a virtue if you have it not. Let me think you're running

straight, even if you're not.   You went off the lines yesterday—go off 'em again to-day, only don't go and cackle
about it, and don't blush to talk like a decent woman.   The
time and place invite, we'll say; and you really feel as if you
must.   Well then, let yourself go completely; do everything
you can think of; fling modesty to the winds; but only while
you're there.   When you come away, no more naughtiness.
Let your doings be buried under the bedclothes.   But while
you *are* there, slip off your chemise without a blush and let
him get his thigh well over yours.   And let him thrust his
tongue as far as it will go into your coral mouth and let passion prompt you to all manner of pretty devices.   Talk lovingly.   Say all sorts of naughty things, and let the bed creak
and groan as you writhe with pleasure.   But as soon as you
have got your things on again, look the nice demure little
lady you ought to be, and let your modesty belie your wan-
tonness.   Bamboozle society, bamboozle me; but don't let
me know it, that's all; and let me go on living in my fool's
paradise.

Why are you for ever sending and receiving letters under
my very nose?   Why is your bed creased and crumpled in
every direction?   How is it your hair is in such a tousled
state?   You don't get it like that in your sleep; and that
mark on your neck there, as though some one had had his
teeth in it, what's that?   Very soon you'll be at it under my
very eyes.   If you don't care what people say and think
about you, be a little thoughtful about me.   I feel like crum-
pling up altogether every time you come and tell me these
things.   I feel as if my blood had all turned to ice.   Then
how I love!   And how I try to hate what I can't help loving;
then I wish I was dead, but with you dead beside me.

I shan't do any spying; I shan't keep on at you, when I
see you ready to deny my charge.   Your disavowal shall be
your innocence.   And even if I catch you in the act, even

if I see you with my very eyes, just tell me it wasn't so and your words shall be more convincing than my eyes. It will be easy enough for you to vanquish a foe who only asks to be vanquished. But don't, oh, don't, forget to let your tongue say "not guilty." When you can win so easily with those two words, well—just win, if not by the merits of your cause, at all events by the softness of your judge.

ELEGY XV

HE BIDS FAREWELL TO HIS WANTON MUSE, TO COURT ONE MORE AUSTERE

SEEK a new Poet, mother of tender Loves. I'm now rounding the last mark with my elegies. Those songs which I, a child of the Pelignian countryside, have written, have been a delight to me and they have not put me to shame. If it's anything to boast about, my title of Knight is an old ancestral one. I'm not a parvenu of the latest war. Mantua delights in Virgil, Verona in Catullus; I shall be called the glory of the Pelignians, of the people who so loved freedom that they did not hesitate to fight and die for it when Rome was menaced by confederate hosts. Some day when he sees Sulmo of many streams, close girdled by her narrow ramparts, the traveler will exclaim, "Little town, for all thy littleness, I'll call thee great, because thou wast able to produce so great a poet."

Lovely boy, and thou, Venus, his mother, pluck from my fields your golden standards. The god of the hornèd brow, Lyæus, hath struck me with a mightier thyrsus, and bids me urge my steeds over a wider plain. Farewell, ye dainty elegies, and thou, my kindly Muse, farewell; when I am gone, my work will still live on.

THE ART OF LOVE

BOOK I

IF there be any one among you who is ignorant of the art of loving, let him read this poem and, having read it and acquired the knowledge it contains, let him address himself to Love.

By art the swift ships are propelled with sail and oar; there is art in driving the fleet chariots, and Love should by art be guided. Automedon was a skilled charioteer and knew how to handle the flowing reins; Tiphys was the pilot of the good ship Argo. I have been appointed by Venus as tutor to tender Love. I shall be known as the Tiphys and Automedon of Love. Love is somewhat recalcitrant and ofttimes refuses to do my bidding; but 'tis a boy, and boys are easily molded. Chiron brought up the boy Achilles to the music of the lyre, and by that peaceful art softened his wild nature; he, before whom his enemies were destined so oft to tremble, who many a time struck terror even into his own companions was, so 'tis said, timid and submissive in the presence of a feeble old man, obedient to his master's voice, and held out to him for chastisement those hands whereof Hector was one day destined to feel the weight. Chiron was tutor to Achilles; I am tutor to Love; both of them formidable youngsters, both of them goddess-born. But the fiery bull has to submit to the yoke; the mettled steed vainly champs at the curb that masters him. I, too, will bring Love to heel, even though his arrows pierce my breast and he brandish over my head his flaming torch. The keener his arrows, the fiercer his fires, the more they stir me to avenge my wounds.

I shall not try, O Apollo, to convey the notion that it was from thee I learned the art which I impart; no birds came and sang it in my ear. Clio and her sisters appeared not to me, grazing my herds, O Ascra, in thy vales. Experience is my guide; give ear to the adept; true are the things I sing. Mother of Love, smile on my undertaking.

Hence, ye narrow frontlets, insignia of chastity, and ye trailing robes that half conceal the feet. I sing of love where danger is not; I sing permitted pilferings; free of all offense my verses are.

You, who for the first time are taking up arms beneath the standard of Venus, find out, in the first place, the woman you are fain to love. Your next task will be to bend her to your will; your third to safeguard that your love shall endure. This is my plan, my syllabus. This is the course my chariot will pursue; such is the goal that it will endeavor to attain.

Now, that you still are fancy-free, now is the time for you to choose a woman and say to her: "You are the only woman that I care for." She's not going to be wafted down to you from heaven on the wings of the wind. You must use your own eyes to discover the girl that suits you. The hunter knows where to spread his nets in order to snare the stag; he knows the valley where the wild boar has his lair. The birdcatcher knows where he should spread his line; and the fisherman, what waters most abound in fish. And thou who seekest out the object of a lasting love, learn to know the places which the fair ones most do haunt. You won't have to put to sea in order to do that, or to undertake any distant journeys. Perseus may bring home his Andromeda from sun-scorched India, and the Phrygian swain may go to Greece to bear away his bride; Rome alone will give you a choice of such lovely women, and so many of them, that you will be forced to confess that she gathers within her own bosom all the treasures that the world can show. As numerous as the ears of corn on Gargarus, grapes in Methymna, fish in the ocean, birds in the thickets, stars in the heavens, so numerous are the beautiful girls you'll find in Rome:

Venus has made her seat of empire the city of her beloved Æneas.

If your tastes incline to a young beauty, in the very flower of girlhood, a really inexperienced girl will offer herself to your gaze; if you prefer one rather more mature, there are hundreds of young women who will take your fancy: 'twill be a veritable *embarras de richesses*. But perhaps you would rather have some one still older, still more experienced. In that case you've got a yet larger number to choose from. When the sun begins to enter the sign of the Lion, you've only got to take a stroll beneath the cool shade of Pompey's portico, or near that building adorned with foreign marbles erected by a loving mother who united her offerings to those of a dutiful son. Omit not to visit that portico which, adorned with ancient pictures, is called the portico of Livia, after its foundress. There you will see the Danaides plotting the death of their unhappy kinswomen, and their fell sire grasping in his hand a naked sword. And do not miss the festival of Adonis, mourned of Venus, and the rites celebrated every seventh day by the Syrian Jews.

Shun not the Temple of the Cow of Memphis, who persuades so many women to play the part she played to Jupiter. Even the Forum, strange though it sound, is propitious to love-making. Lawyers are by no means proof against the fiery shafts of Love. Hard by the marble temple sacred to Venus, where play the waters of the Appian fount, many an advocate has fallen a victim to the snares of Love; for the man who defends his client cannot always defend himself. In such a pass, words sometimes fail even the most learned orator. The tables are turned and he finds himself obliged to plead his own cause. From her temple close at hand, Venus laughs to see him in such a quandary. A patron but a little while ago, he would now rejoice to be a client.

But it is especially at the theater you should lay your

snares; that is where you may hope to have your desires fulfilled. Here you will find women to your taste: one for a moment's dalliance, another to fondle and caress, another to have all for your own. Even as the ants that come and go in long battalions with their stores of food, or as the bees, when they have found plants to plunder of their honey, hover hither and thither among the thyme and the flowers, so, and no less numerous, you may see crowds of lovely women, gayly dressed, hastening away to the theater. I have often found it difficult to choose from such a galaxy. They come to see and, more important still, to be seen! The theater's the place where modesty gets a fall.

It was you, Romulus, who first mingled the cares of love with public games, that far-off day when the rape of the Sabine women gave wives to your warriors who had waited for them so long. No curtains then hung in the marble theater, nor was the stage made red with liquid saffron. In those days branches from the woods of the Palatine were the only adornment of our simple stage. The people sat on seats of turf, their heads canopied with boughs.

As soon as he had sat him down, each Roman looked about, marking the woman whom he most desired, giving free play to the thoughts that surged within him. Whilst to the sound of a rustic pipe an actor strikes his foot three times upon the leveled earth, amid the unforced applause of the expectant throng (for in those days applause was neither bought nor sold), Romulus signed to his men to seize upon their prey. In a trice, with shouts that made their object clear, they laid their eager hands upon the cowering women. Even as the weak and timid doves flee before an eagle, even as a young lamb quails at the sight of a wolf, so shuddered the Sabine women when they beheld these fierce warriors making towards them. Every one turned pale, terror spread throughout the throng, but it showed itself in different ways. Some tore their hair; some swooned away; some wept in silence; some called vainly for their mothers; some sobbed aloud; others seemed stupefied with fear; some stood transfixed; others tried to flee. Nevertheless, the Romans carry off the women, sweet booty for their beds, and to many of them, terror lends an added charm.

If one shows herself too rebellious and refuses to follow her ravisher, he picks her up and, pressing her lovingly to his bosom, exclaims, "Why with tears do you thus dim the lovely radiance of your eyes? What your father is to your mother, that will I be to you." O Romulus, you are the only one who has ever known how to reward his soldiers; for such pay, I would willingly enroll myself beneath your banners. Ever since those days, the theaters, faithful to this ancient custom, have always been a dangerous lure to loveliness.

Forget not the arena where mettled steeds strive for the palm of Victory. This circus, where an immense concourse of people is gathered, is very favorable to Love. There, if you would express the secret promptings of your heart, there is no need for you to talk upon your fingers, or to watch for signs to tell you what is in your fair one's mind. Sit close beside her, as close as you are able; there's nothing to prevent. The narrowness of the space compels you to press against her and, fortunately for you, compels her to acquiesce. Then, of course, you must think of some means of starting the conversation. Begin by saying the sort of thing people generally do say on such occasions. Some horses are seen entering the stadium; ask her the name of their owner; and whoever she favors, you should follow suit. And when the solemn procession of the country's gods and goddesses passes along, be sure and give a rousing cheer for Venus, your protectress. If, as not infrequently befalls, a speck of dust lights on your fair one's breast, flick it off with an airy finger;

and if there's nothing there, flick it off just the same; anything is good enough to serve as a pretext for paying her attention. Is her dress dragging on the ground? Gather it up, and take special care that nothing soils it. Perchance, to reward you for your kindness, she'll grant you the favor of letting you see her leg. And then again, you must keep an eye on the people seated in the row behind and see that no one thrusts his knee into her soft shoulders. The merest trifle is enough to win these butterfly ladies. Why, hosts of men have succeeded with a woman merely by the attentive manner in which they have arranged a cushion for her, or fanned her with a fan, or put a stool beneath her dainty feet. Both the circus and the forum afford opportunities for a love-affair. Love often delights to try his strength there, and many a man, who came to see another wounded, finds that he has been pinked himself. While he is talking and stroking her hand, asking for the race-card and, having put his money on, is inquiring what has won, an arrow pierces him before he knows where he is; he heaves a sigh and, instead of being a mere spectator of the combat, he finds himself a victim.

Did we not see this happen quite recently, when Cæsar offered us the spectacle of a sea-fight showing the Persian and the Athenian ships in action. Then indeed, from both seas, youths and maidens flocked to see the show and the whole world was gathered within the City. Which of us, in that vast throng, found not a woman worthy of his love; and, alas, how many were tortured by a foreign flame.

But lo, Cæsar makes ready to complete the conquest of the world! Ye far-off countries of the East, to our laws shall ye submit; and you, ye arrogant Parthians, shall be punished as ye deserve. Rejoice, shades of Crassus, and you, ye Roman Eagles, ashamed at your long sojourn in barbarian hands, be of good cheer, your avenger is at hand. Scarce has

he essayed to wield his arms, and yet he proves himself a
skillful leader. Though he himself is but a boy, he wages
a war unsuited to his boyish years. O, ye of little faith, vex
not your souls about the age of the gods! Courage in a
Cæsar does not wait upon the years. Genius divine outpaces
time and brooks not the tedium of tardy growth. Hercules
was still no more than a child when he crushed the serpents
in his baby hands. Even in the cradle he proved himself a
worthy son of Jove. And you, Bacchus, still glowing with
youthful radiance, how mighty wast thou when India trembled at thy conquering Thyrsi! With the auspices and with
the courage of thy sire shalt thou wield thine arms, young
Cæsar; with the courage and with the auspices of thy sire
shalt thou overthrow thine enemies. Such a beginning becomes the name thou bearest. To-day thou art Prince of
the Youths; one day thou shalt be Prince of the Elders.
Since thou hast brothers, avenge thy slaughtered brethren;
and since thou hast a sire, defend thy father's rights. It is
thy father, thy country's father, who hath armed thee, what
time the foe is violently wrestling the scepter from a parent's
struggling hand. Thy sacred cause shall triumph o'er the
perjured foe; justice and piety shall march beneath thy standards. The righteousness of our cause shall overcome the
Parthians; arms shall drive the victory home, and so to
Latium's riches, the wealth of the Orient shall my young
hero add. Mars, his sire, and thou Cæsar, his sire too, a god
the one, the other soon a god to be, watch over him and
keep him from all harm. I can read the hidden secrets of
the future. Aye, thou wilt conquer. I will sing thy glory
in verses consecrate to thee; with a loud voice I will sound
thy praise. Standing erect will I depict thee, and urging thy
warriors to the combat. Grant that my song be not unworthy of the prowess that it celebrates! I will sing of the
Parthian turning to flee, and of the Roman facing the arrows

aimed at him by the flying foe. What, Parthian, dost thou
leave to the conquered, who seekest victory in flight? Henceforth, for thee Mars forebodeth nought but ill.

  That day shall dawn, O fairest of mankind, when, resplendent with gold, by four white horses drawn, thou shalt
pass within the City walls. Before thee, laden with chains,
shall walk the conquered leaders; nor shall they then, as erst
they did, seek safety in flight. Young men and maidens shall
with joy behold the sight, and with gladness shall all hearts
be filled. Then if some fair one shall ask of thee the name
of this or that defeated monarch, what all these emblems
mean, what country this, what mountain that, or what that
river yonder represents, answer at once, anticipate her ques-
tions, speak up with confidence, and even when your mind's
a blank, speak up as if you had the knowledge pat. "Here's
the Euphrates, with his sedgy crown; and that old fellow
there, with sky-blue hair, why, he's the Tigris; and those?
. . . hum! . . . well, they're Armenians. That woman
yonder? She is Persia, where the son of Danaë was born.
That town till lately rose up amid the vales of Achæmenes.
That prisoner there, or that other one yonder? Oh, they
are captured generals." And if you know them, give their
names. If you don't, invent them.

  Dinners and banquets offer easy access to women's favor,
and the pleasures of the grape are not the only entertainment
you may find there; Love, with rosy cheeks, often presses in
her frail hands the amphora of Bacchus. As soon as his wings
are drenched with wine, Cupid grows drowsy and stirs not
from his place. But anon he'll be up and shaking the moisture from his wings, and woe betide the man or woman
who receives a sprinkling of this burning dew. Wine fills
the heart with thoughts of love and makes it prompt to
catch on fire. All troubles vanish, put to flight by copious
draughts. Then is the time for laughter, the poor man

plucks up courage and imagines he's a millionaire. To the deuce with worries and troubles! Brows unpucker and hearts expand; every tongue's inspired by frankness, and calls a spade a spade. We've often lost our heart to a pretty girl at dinner. Bringing love and wine together is adding fuel to fire indeed. Don't judge a woman by candle-light, it's deceptive. If you really want to know what she's like, look at her by daylight, and when you're sober. It was broad daylight, and under the open sky, that Paris looked upon the three goddesses and said to Venus, "You are lovelier than your two rivals." Night covers a multitude of blemishes and imperfections. At night there is no such thing as an ugly woman! If you want to look at precious stones, or colored cloth, you take them out into the light of day; and it's by daylight you should judge a woman's face and figure.

But if I'm to mention all the places favorable to woman-hunting, I might as well attempt to number the sands of the seashore. Of course, there's Baiæ, with white sails gleaming out in the bay, and its hot sulphur spring. Many a bather, who has gone there for his health, comes away saying, "Those precious baths are not such healthy things as people make out." Not far from the gates of Rome, behold the temple of Diana shaded by trees, the scene of many a hard-fought contest for the prize of Love. Because she's a virgin and hates the darts of Love, Diana has inflicted many a wound there, and will inflict many more.

Thus far my Muse, borne in her chariot with wheels of different height, has told you, would-be lover, where to seek your prey, and how to lay your snares. Now I'll teach you how to captivate and hold the woman of your choice. This is the most important part of all my lessons. Lovers of every land, lend an attentive ear to my discourse; let goodwill warm your hearts, for I am going to fulfill the promises I made you.

First of all, be quite sure that there isn't a woman who

cannot be won, and make up your mind that you will win her. Only you must prepare the ground. Sooner would the birds cease their song in the springtime, or the grasshopper be silent in the summer, or the hare turn and give chase to a hound of Mænalus, than a woman resist the tender wooing of a youthful lover. Perhaps you think she doesn't want to yield. You're wrong. She wants to, in her heart of hearts. Stolen love is just as sweet to women as it is to us. Man is a poor dissembler; woman is much more skillful in concealing her desire. If all the men agreed that they would never more make the first advance, the women would soon be fawning at our feet. Out in the springy meadow the heifer lows with longing for the bull; the mare neighs at the approach of the stallion. With men and women love is more restrained, and passion is less fierce. They keep within bounds. Need I mention Byblis, who burned for her brother with an incestuous flame, and hanged herself to expiate her crime? Or Myrrha, who loved her father, but not as a father should be loved, and now her shame is hidden by the bark of the tree that covered her. O sweetly scented tree, the tears which she distills, to us give perfume and recall the ill-fated maid's unhappy name.

One day in wood-crowned Ida's shady vale, a white bull went wandering by. The pride of all the herd was he. Between his horns was just a single spot of black; save for that mark, his body was as white as milk; and all the heifers of Gnossus and of Cydonia sighed for the joy of his caress Pasiphaë conceived a passion for him and viewed with jealous eye the loveliest among the heifers. There's no gainsaying it, Crete with her hundred cities, Crete, liar though she be, cannot deny it. 'Tis said that Pasiphaë, with hands unused to undertake such toil, tore from the trees their tenderest shoots, culled from the meadows bunches of sweet grass and hastened to offer them to her beloved bull. Whithersoever

he went, she followed him; nothing would stay her. She recked not of her spouse; the bull had conquered Minos. "What avails it, Pasiphaë, to deck yourself in costly raiment? How can your lover of such riches judge? Wherefore, mirror in hand, dost thou follow the wandering herd up to the mountain top? Wherefore dost thou for ever range thy hair? Look in thy mirror: 'twill tell thee thou art no meet mistress for a bull. Ah, what wouldst thou not have given if Nature had but armed thy brow with horns! If Minos still doth hold a corner in thy heart, cease this adulterous love; or if thou must deceive thy spouse, at least deceive him with a man." She hearkens not, but, fleeing from his royal couch, she ranges ever on and on, through forest after forest, like to a Bacchante full of the spirit that unceasingly torments her. How often, looking with jealous anger on a heifer, did she exclaim, "How then can she find favor in his sight? See how she prances before him on the green. Fool, she doubtless deems that thus she is lovelier in his eyes." Then, at her command, the hapless beast is taken from the herd and sent to bow her head beneath the yoke; or else, pretending to offer sacrifice to the gods, she orders her to be slain at the altar; and then with joy fingers o'er the entrails of her rival. How often, under the guise of one who offers sacrifice, hath she appeased the alleged displeasure of the gods, and waving the bleeding trophies in her hand exclaimed, "Go, get thee to my lover, please him now!" Now she would be Europa; now she would be Io; the one because she was a heifer, the other because a bull bore her on his back. Howbeit, deceived by the image of a cow of maple wood, the king of the herd performed with her the act of love, and by the offspring was the sire betrayed.

Had that other Cretan girl been able to forego her passion for Thyestes (but how hard it is for a woman to love one man alone), Phœbus would not have been compelled to stay his steeds in mid-career, and to have driven his chariot back again towards the Dawn. The daughter of Nisus, because she had stolen from the father's head the fatal lock of hair, is evermore beset by ravening dogs. The son of Atreus, though he escaped the perils of the battlefield and the ocean, died beneath the dagger of his cruel spouse. Who has listened dry-eyed to the love story of Creusa? Who has not hated the mad fury of Medea, a mother stained with her children's blood? Phœnix, the son of Amyntor, wept with his sightless orbs. You, ye steeds, in your terror, tore Hippolytus in pieces. Wherefore, Phineus, didst thou put out the eyes of thy innocent sons? Upon thine own head will that punishment return.

Such are the consequences of woman's unbridled passion. Fiercer it is than ours, with more of frenzy in it.

Be, then, of good cheer, and never doubt that you will conquer. Not one woman in a thousand will seriously resist. Whether a pretty woman grants or withholds her favors, she always likes to be asked for them. Even if you are repulsed, you don't run any danger. But why should a woman refuse? People don't resist the temptation of new delights. We always deem that other people are more fortunate than ourselves. The crop is always better in our neighbor's field; his cows more rich in milk.

Now the first thing you have to do is to get on good terms with the fair one's maid. She can make things easy for you. Find out whether she is fully in her mistress's confidence, and if she knows all about her secret dissipations. Leave no stone unturned to win her over. Once you have her on your side, the rest is easy. Let her watch for a favorable time (that's a precaution that doctors do not neglect); let her take advantage of the moment when her mistress may more easily be persuaded, when she is more likely to surrender to a lover's solicitations. At such times, the whole

world seems *couleur de rose* to her; gayety dances in her
eyes as the golden wheat-ears dance in a fertile field. When
the heart is glad, when it is not gripped by sorrow, it opens
and expands. Then it is that Love slips gently into its inmost folds. So long as Ilion was plunged in mourning, her
warriors kept the Greeks at bay; it was when she was re-
joicing and making merry that she received within her walls
the fatal horse with its armèd freight. Choose, too, the moment when your charmer is smarting from the insult of a
rival; make her see in you a means of wiping off the score.
When, in the morning, she is doing her mistress's hair, let
the maid foment her anger, let her press on with sail and
oar and, sighing, murmur, "Why not, Madam, pay him out
in his own coin?" Then let her talk of you; let her adroitly
sing your praises and swear that you, poor fellow, are wildly
in love with her. But don't lose any time, for fear the wind
should drop and the sails hang limp. Fragile as ice, a woman's
anger is a transient thing.

"What about the maid herself?" you ask. "Is it well to
win her favors first?" Now that's a ticklish business. Sometimes it stimulates their zeal; sometimes the opposite's the
case. One girl will do her utmost for her mistress, another
will want to keep you for herself. The only thing is just
to try, and see how it turns out. On the whole, my advice
to you is "Don't." I shouldn't risk these steep and dangerous
byways myself. If you keep with me, you'll be on the right
road. If, however, you are taken with the servant's charms,
if you find her as pretty as she's zealous, win the mistress
first, and afterwards turn your attention to the maid; but
don't begin with her. Only I warn you, if you have any
faith in my teaching, if my words are not dispersed by the
winds over the seas, don't make the attempt at all unless you
carry it right through. Once she herself is well involved,
she won't give *you* away. The bird, with its wings well

limed, won't fly far; the boar can't escape from the nets; once a fish is on the hook, he can't get away. So my advice to you is, push your attack well home, and don't be in a hurry to withdraw your forces when the victory's won. Thus she'll be your companion in crime, and she'll never betray you; she'll tell you everything you want to know about her mistress. The great thing is to be careful. If you keep your goings-on with the maid quite dark, you'll hear about everything her mistress does.

Some people think that time and the seasons only concern farmers and seafaring men. They're wrong. Just as there's a time to sow, and a time to sail, so there's a time to begin on a pretty girl. Success often depends on your seizing the right moment to open the attack. Keep clear of her birthday, for example, and shun the Kalends of March. Don't begin when there's a big show on at the circus. That would prove the winter of your discontent, when the stormy winds would blow, and you'd do well to hold off. If you launch the ship then, you'll be lucky if you're washed ashore clinging to a spar. If you want a really good opportunity, wait for the anniversary of the fatal day when Roman blood incarnadined the waters of the Allia, or for that one day out of the seven on which the Syrian Jew will do no manner of work. Above all, don't go near her on her birthday; or indeed on any day when you're expected to give a present. However much you try to wriggle out of it, she'll make you buy her something. A woman always knows how to exploit an ardent lover. Some peddler fellow will be sure to turn up, and since buying's a mania with them all, she'll be sure to find the very things she wants. She'll ask you to look at 'em; then she'll kiss you, and say, "Oh, do buy me that. It'll last for years; it's just the very thing I want, and you couldn't buy me anything I should like more." It's no good saying you haven't got the money on you; she'll ask

you to draw a check, and then you'll curse the day you
learned to write. And how many times you'll have to give
her something for her birthday! Every time she wants anything very special, she'll have a birthday. And then she'll
come grieving some pretended loss; she'll come to you with
eyes all read with weeping and tell you she's lost one of her
precious ear-rings. That's the little game they play. Then
they'll keep on asking you to lend them money; and once
they've got it, I wouldn't give much for your chances of
getting it back. You can look on that as gone, and they
won't give you so much as a "thank you." Why, if I'd got
ten mouths and ten tongues, I couldn't tell you all the tricks
our ladies of the *demi-monde* get up to.

In the first place, it's best to send her a letter, just to pave
the way. In it you should tell her how you dote on her;
pay her pretty compliments and say all the nice things lovers
always say. Achilles gave way to Priam's supplications.
Even the gods are moved by the voice of entreaty. And
promise, promise, promise. Promises will cost you nothing.
Every one's a millionaire where promises are concerned.
Hope, if only she is duly fostered, holds out a long time.
She's a deceitful goddess, but a very useful one. If you
give your mistress something, she may give you your *congé*.
She will have had her *quid pro quo*. Always make her think
you're just about to give, but never really do so. Thus your
farmer will keep on manuring a barren field, hoping it will
produce a crop some day. Your gambler will keep throw-
ing good money after bad, in hopes of redeeming all his losses;
and thus his greed falls a victim to his hope of gain. The
really great problem, the problem that takes all a man's skill
to solve, is to win a woman's favors without making her a
present. If you succeed in that, she will go on giving, so
as not to lose the guerdon of the favors she has already bestowed. So send off your letter and couch it in the sweetest

terms; it should be a sort of preliminary reconnaissance and pave the way to her heart. A few characters written on an apple led the young Cydippe astray and, when she had read them, the rash girl found she was ensnared by her own words.

Take my advice, my youthful fellow-citizens, and study the fine arts, not only that you may champion the cause of some trembling dependent. The common herd, the austere judge, and those superior people, the senators, are not the only people who are moved by eloquence. But don't show your hand, and don't be in too much of a hurry to display your powers of speech. And don't put on the professorial style. Who but an idiot would write to his mistress as though he were addressing a meeting. A show-off letter will often turn a woman against you. Be quite natural, quite simple, but engaging. In a word, say just what you would say if you were speaking to her. If she refuses your letter and sends it back unread, don't give up; hope for the best and try again. The unruly bull bows to the yoke in time, and, in time, the most obstreperous colt gets broken in. You can wear through an iron ring by continuous friction; the plow-share wears away every day against the soil it cleaves. What could you have harder than a rock, or less hard than water? Nevertheless, water will wear away the hardest rock. So keep pegging away, and, given time, you'll get your way with Penelope herself. Troy held out a long time, but it fell at last. Suppose she reads your letter but doesn't answer. So be it. Only keep her busy reading. Since she has condescended to read, she'll answer some fine day. Everything comes gradually and at its appointed hour. Peradventure she'll write in a huff and tell you to cease annoying her. If she does, she's trembling lest you take her at her word. She wants you to go on, although she tells you not to. So go on, and soon you'll have your heart's desire.

If you see your mistress being borne along on her litter,

go up to her as if by accident, and say what you've got to say in vague ambiguous language, for fear some busybody should be listening. If you see her hanging about under some portico, as if she didn't know what to do with herself, go and walk there too. Sometimes get in front of her, and sometimes drop behind. Don't be bashful about getting clear of the crowd and crossing over to her side. Don't, on any account, let her go to the theater, looking her loveliest, without your being there to see. Her bare shoulders will give you something charming to contemplate. And you can look at her and admire her at your leisure; and speak to her with eyes and gestures. Applaud the actor that plays the girl's part; applaud still more the man that plays the lover. If she stands up, stand up too; and while she is sitting, keep your seat; don't worry about the time, squander it as your mistress may require.

And don't, for heaven's sake, have your hair waved, or use powder on your skin. Leave such foppishness as that to the effeminate priests who wail their Phrygian chants in honor of Cybele. Simplicity in dress is what best befits a man. Theseus conquered Ariadne without troubling about the way his hair was done. Phædra fell in love with Hippolytus, who certainly was not a dandy. Adonis, a simple woodlander, was the idol of a goddess. Study to be clean, let your skin be tanned in the open air, wear well-cut clothes, and see there are no spots on them. Have a clean tongue, and let your teeth be free from tartar; and don't slop about in boots that are two or three sizes too big for you.

Don't let your hair stick up in tufts on your head; see that your hair and your beard are decently trimmed. See also that your nails are clean and nicely filed; don't have any hair growing out of your nostrils; take care that your breath is sweet, and don't go about reeking like a billy-goat. All other toilet refinements leave to the women or to perverts.

But lo, Bacchus is summoning his bard; propitious to lovers, he fosters the fires with which he is consumed himself. Ariadne was wandering distraught along the lonely wave-beaten shores of Naxos. Scarce had sleep departed from her eyes, and she wore but an airy shift; her feet were bare and her fair tresses were blowing about her shoulders. To the heedless billows she was crying wildly for her Theseus, and tears flowed in torrents down her cheeks. She cried aloud and wept at the same time. But both enhanced her beauty. "Oh, the faithless one," she cried, beating her tender bosom again and again, "he has abandoned me. Oh, what will become of me! What will be my fate!" She spake. And on a sudden, drums and cymbals beaten and tossed by frenzied hands resounded along the shore. Stricken with terror, she fell gasping out a few broken words, and the blood faded from her lifeless corse. But lo, the Mænads, with their hair floating wildly out behind them, and the light-footed Satyrs, the rout that leads the procession of Apollo, came upon the scene. Behold, old Silenus, reeling-ripe as usual, who can scarce keep his seat on the ass that staggers beneath the heavy burden. He pursues the Mænads, who flee from him and mock him as they flee, and as he belabors his long-eared beast with his staff, the unskillful cavalier tumbles head-foremost from his steed. And all the Satyrs shout, "Up with you, old man Silenus, up with you again!"

Meanwhile from his lofty chariot with vine branches all bedecked, the god, handling the golden reins, drives on his team of tigers. The girl, in losing Theseus, had lost her color and her voice. Thrice she attempted flight, thrice did fear paralyze her steps; she shuddered, she trembled like the tapering stem or the slender reed that sways at the slightest breath. "Banish all thy fears," cried the god. "In me thou findest a tenderer, more faithful lover than Theseus. Daughter of Minos, thou shalt be the bride of Bacchus. Thy guerdon shall be a dwelling in the sky; thou shalt be a new star and thy bright diadem shall be a guide to the pilot uncertain of his course." So saying he leapt from his chariot lest his tigers should affright her. The sand yielded beneath his feet. Clasping to his breast the swooning, unresisting girl, he bore her away. For a god may do as he wills, and who shall say him nay. Then some sang *Hymenæe!* and some *Evion Evoë!* and to these strains the god and his bride consummated their spousals on the sacred couch.

When, then, you find yourself at a feast where the wine is flowing freely, and where a woman shares the same couch with you, pray to that god whose mysteries are celebrated during the night, that the wine may not over-cloud thy brain. 'Tis then thou mayest easily hold converse with thy mistress in hidden words whereof she will easily divine the meaning. A drop of wine will enable you to draw sweet emblems on the table wherein she will read the proof of the love you have for her. Fix well thine eyes on her and so confirm the message of thy love. Ofttimes, without a word being spoken, the eyes can tell a wondrous tale. When she has drunk, be thou the first to seize the cup, and where her lips have touched, there press thine own and drink. Choose thou the dainties that her fingers have lightly touched, and as thou reachest for them, let thy hand softly encounter hers.

Be courteous to her husband too. Nothing could better serve your plans than to be in his good graces. If, when the dice are thrown, chance crowns thee king of the feast, yield him the honor; take off thy wreath and place it on his brow. Whether he be thy equal or inferior matters not. Let him be served the first, and flatter him in everything you say. The surest and most common means to success is to deceive him under the cloak of friendship. But though 'tis sure and common, 'tis none the less a crime. Sometimes in love the ambassador goes too far and doth exceed the terms of his mandate.

Now I will lay down the limits thou shouldst observe in drinking: never drink enough to cloud your brain or make your gait unsteady; avoid the quarrels that are born of wine and be not prompt to take offense. Follow not the example of Eurytion, who, like a fool, gave up the ghost because he had drunk too much. The food and the wine should inspire a gentle gayety. If you have a voice, sing; and if your limbs are supple, dance; in short, do everything you can to make a good impression. Downright drunkenness is a loathsome thing; simulated inebriety may serve a useful purpose. Let your tongue falter with a cunning stammer; pretend it's difficult for you to pronounce your words, so that whatever you do or say a little on the risky side may be put down to the fact that you've had too much liquor. Drink to your mistress, and do it openly, and drink to the man that shares her bed—and, under your breath, curse her lawful spouse. When the guests rise up to go, you'll have a good chance to get very close to your lady. Mingle in the crowd, contrive to get near her, press her side with your fingers and rub your foot against hers.

And now, we'll say, you've got her to yourself. Now you can talk to her. Avaunt then, rustic modesty! Fortune and Venus favor the brave. Don't ask me to tell you what to say. Just take and begin, the words will come fast enough without your having to search for them. You must play the lover for all you're worth. Tell her how you are pining for her; do everything you know to win her over. She will believe you fast enough. Every woman thinks herself attractive; even the plainest is satisfied with the charms she deems that she possesses. And, then, how often it has happened that the man who begins by feigning love ends by falling in love in real earnest. Ah, my fair ones, look with indulgent eye on those that give themselves a lover's airs; the love, now feigned, will soon be love indeed.

By subtle flatteries you may be able to steal into her heart, even as the river insensibly o'erflows the banks which fringe it. Never cease to sing the praises of her face, her hair, her taper fingers and her dainty foot. The coldest beauty is moved by praises of her charms, and even the innocent and greenest girl takes pride and pleasure in the care of her good looks. If it were not so, wherefore should Juno and Minerva blush even now to have failed to carry off the prize for loveliness, in the woods of Ida? See that peacock there; if you belaud his plumage, he'll spread his tail with pride; but if in silence you look at him, he'll never show his treasures. The courser, in the chariot race, is proud of the admiration bestowed on his well-groomed mane and his proudly arched neck. Be not backward in your promises; women are drawn on by promises; and swear by all the gods that you'll be as good as your word. Jove, from his high abode, looks down and laughs on lovers' perfidies, and gives them to Æolus for the winds to sport with. Often he swore to Juno by the Styx that he'd be faithful, and he broke his vows. His example should lend us courage.

'Tis well that the gods should exist and well that we should believe in them. Let us bring offerings of wine and frankincense to their immemorial altars. They are not sunk in indolent repose and slothful ease. Live then in innocence, for the gods are omnipresent. Fulfill the trust that has been reposed in you; observe the precepts of religion; have nought to do with fraud; stain not your hands with blood. If you are wise, practice deceit on women alone, for that you may do with impunity; but in all other matters let your word be your bond. Deceive them that are deceivers; women for the most part are a perfidious race; let them fall into the snares which they themselves have prepared. Egypt, so they tell, being deprived of the rains which fertilize its soil, had suffered nine years of continuous drought when Thrasius came to Busiris and announced that Jove could be propitiated by the shedding of a stranger's blood. "Then," said Busiris, "thou shalt be the first victim offered to the god; thou shalt be that stranger-guest to whom Egypt shall owe the rain from heaven." Phalaris, too, caused the ferocious Perillus to be burnt within the brazen bull which he had fashioned, and the ill-fated craftsman was the first to put his handi-work to the proof. Both penalties were just; and indeed there is no law more righteous than that the contrivers of death should perish by their own inventions. Wherefore, since a lie should pay for a lie, let woman be deceived and let her blame no one but herself for the treachery whereof she set the example.

Tears, too, are a mighty useful resource in the matter of love. They would melt a diamond. Make a point, there-fore, of letting your mistress see your face all wet with tears. Howbeit, if you cannot manage to squeeze out any tears—and they won't always flow just when you want them to—put your finger in your eyes. What lover of experience does not know how greatly kisses add cogency to tender speeches? If she refuse to be kissed, kiss her all the same. She may struggle to begin with. "Horrid man!" she'll say; but if she fights, 'twill be a losing battle. Nevertheless, don't be too rough with her and hurt her dainty mouth. Don't give her cause to say that you're a brute. And if, after you've kissed her, you fail to take the rest, you don't de-serve even what you've won. What more did you want to come to the fulfillment of your desires? Oh, shame on you! It was not your modesty, it was your stupid clownishness. You would have hurt her in the struggle, you say? But women like being hurt. What they like to give, they love to be robbed of. Every woman taken by force in a hurricane of passion is transported with delight; nothing you could give her pleases her like that. But when she comes forth scathless from a combat in which she might have been taken by assault, however pleased she may try to look, she is sorry in her heart. Phœbe was raped, and so, too, was her sister Elaira; and yet they loved their ravishers not a whit the less.

A well-known story, but one that may well be told again, is that of Achilles and the maid of Scyros. Venus had rewarded Paris for the homage he had paid to her beauty when at the foot of Mount Ida she triumphed over her two rivals. From a far-off country a new daughter-in-law has come to Priam, and within the walls of Ilion there dwells an Argive bride. The Greeks swore to avenge the outraged husband; for an affront to one was an affront to all. Howbeit, Achilles (shame on him if he had not yielded to a mother's prayers) had disguised his manhood beneath the garments of a girl. "What dost thou there, descendant of Æacus? Dost thou busy thyself with carding wool? Is that a task for a man? It is by other arts of Pallas that thou shouldst seek for fame. What hast thou to do with work-baskets? Thine arm is made to bear the shield. How comes this distaff in the hand that should lay Hector low? Cast from thee these spindles, and let thy doughty hand brandish a spear from Pelion." Once chance brought Achilles and the royal maiden together in the same bedchamber, and then the onslaught she underwent swiftly revealed to her the sex of her companion. Doubtless she yielded only to superior force; so we must of course believe; but at least she was not angry that force gained the day. "Stay yet awhile," she said entreatingly, when Achilles, eager to be gone, had laid aside the distaff to seize his valiant arms. What then has become of this alleged violence? Wherefore, Deidamia, wilt thou retain with pleading tones the author of thy downfall?

True, if modesty does not permit a woman to make the first advance, it nevertheless delights her to yield when her lover takes the initiative. In truth a lover reposes too much confidence in his good looks if he thinks that a woman will be the first to ask. 'Tis for him to begin, for him to entreat her; and to his supplications she will incline her ear. Ask and thou shalt receive; she only waits to be implored. Tell her the cause and origin of your desire. Jove bent the knee to the heroines of old times, and for all his greatness, none ever came of her own accord to entreat him. If, however, you only get disdain for all your pains, draw back and press your suit no farther. Many women long for what eludes them, and like not what is offered them. Cool off; don't let her think you too importunate. Do not betray the hope of too swift a victory; let Love steal in disguised as Friendship. I've often seen a woman thus disarmed, and friendship ripen into love.

A pale complexion ill becomes a sailor. The rays of the sun and the salt spray should have tanned his features; nor does it suit the husbandman who, with plow or heavy rakes, is for ever turning up the soil in the open air; and ye who strive for the athlete's crown of olive, it would ill beseem you to have too white a skin. But every lover should be pale; pallor is the symptom of Love, it is the hue appropriate to Love. So, deceived by your paleness, let your mistress be tenderly solicitous for your health. Orion was pale with love when he wandered after Lyrice in the woods of Dirce. Pale, too, was Daphnis for the Naiad that disdained him. Thinness, too, is an index to the feelings; and be not ashamed to veil your shining hair beneath the hood. Sleepless nights make thin a young man's body. So that thou mayest come to the fruition of your desires, shrink not from exciting pity, that all who behold you may exclaim, "Why, poor wretch, you are in love." Shall I complain aloud or only whisper it,

how virtue is on every side confounded with vice? Friendship and constancy are both but empty names. You cannot
with safety tell your friend all the charms of the woman you
adore; if he believed what you said of her, he would straightway become your rival. But, you will argue, the grandson
of Actor stained not the couch of Achilles; Phædra erred not.
at least, not in favor of Pirithoüs; Pylades loved Hermione
with a love as chaste as that which Phœbus bore for Pallas,
or as the love of Castor and Pollux for their sister Helen.
But if you count on miracles like that, you might as well
expect to cull apples from the tamarisk, or to gather honey
in the middle of a river. Vice is so inviting, and each man
seeks but to gratify his own pleasure. And pleasure is sweetest when 'tis paid for by another's pain. Shun those men
you think you can rely on, and you'll be safe. Beware alike
of kinsman, brother, and dear friend. They are the people
who generally make the trouble.

I was on the point of ending here; but let me add that
women are things of many moods. You must adapt your
treatment to the special case. The same soil is not equally
good for everything. This land is good for the vine, and
this for olives; and here's the place for corn. You'll find
as many dispositions in the world as you meet with different
figures and faces. A clever man will know how to adapt
himself to this diversity of temper and disposition, and suit
his conversation to the needs of the hour, even as Proteus,
who is now a graceful wave, now a lion, now a tree, and now
a boar with bristling hide. It's the same with fish; some
you spear, others you take with the line, and others again in
the encircling net. Different methods suit different people.
You must vary them according to the age of your mistresses.
An old hind will descry your machinations from afar. If
you display too much skill to the novice, and too much
enterprise to the bashful, you'll frighten her and put her

on her guard. Thus it sometimes happens that a woman, who has feared to yield to the caresses of a man of breeding, will fall into the arms of a worthless knave.

A part of my enterprise is now achieved, though more remains behind. Here then let us heave the anchor and give ourselves a little rest.

THE ART OF LOVE

BOOK II

SING, and sing again Io Pæan! The quarry that I was hot upon hath fallen into my toils. Let the joyous lover set the laurel crown upon my brow and raise me to a loftier pinnacle than Hesiod of Ascra or the blind old bard of Mæonia. Thus did Priam's son, crowding on all sail in his flight from war-like Amyclæ, bear with him his ravished bride; and thus, too, Hippodamia, did Pelops, in his victorious chariot, carry thee far from thy native land.

Young man, why wilt thou haste so fast? Thy vessel sails the open sea, and the harbor to which I am steering thee is still far off. It sufficeth not that my verses have brought thy mistress to thine arms; my art hath taught thee how to win her; it must also teach thee how to keep her. Though it be glorious to make conquests, it is still more glorious to retain them. The former is sometimes the work of chance, the latter is always the work of skill.

Queen of Cythera, and thou her son, if ever ye looked with kindly eye upon me, 'tis, above all, to-day that of your succor I have need. And thee too, Erato, I invoke, for 'tis from love thou dost derive thy name. Great is the enterprise I have in mind. I am going to tell how Love, that fickle child, may captured be; Love that is wandering up and down in this wide world of ours. Airy is he, possessed of wings to fly withal. How shall we stay his flight?

Minos had left no stone unturned to prevent the escape of his stranger-guest. Yet he dared, with wings, to cleave himself a way. When Dædalus had imprisoned the monster half-man, half-bull, that his erring mother had conceived, he spoke to Minos saying, "O thou who art so just, set a term to my exile; let my native land receive my ashes. If the Fates forbid that I should live in my own country, grant at

least that I may die there. Grant that my son may return
to his home, even if his father beseeches thee in vain. Or
if thou hast no pity for the child, let thy compassion light
upon the father." Thus spake Dædalus; but in vain he tried
with these and many other words like these, to touch the
heart of Minos; inexorable, he was deaf to all his prayers.
Seeing his supplications were of no avail, he said to himself,
"Behold, here is indeed a chance for thee to prove thy ingenuity. Minos rules the land, and rules the waves; 'tis useless then on sea or land to seek escape. There remains the
air; and through the air I'll cleave me a way. Great Jove,
pardon the rashness of my undertaking. 'Tis not my aim to
raise myself to the skyish dwellings of the gods; but there
is for me one means, and one alone, whereby I may escape
the tyrant. If there were a way across the Styx, the Stygian
waters I would not fear to cross. Grant me then to change
the laws that rule my nature."

Misfortune ofttimes stimulates invention. Who would
ever have thought a man could voyage through the air!
Nevertheless, 'tis true that Dædalus wrought himself wings
with feathers cunningly disposed like oars, and with thread
did fix his flimsy work together. The lower part he bound
with wax melted by the fire. And now behold the strange
and wondrous work is finished! The boy, with a joyous
smile, handles the feathers and the wax, witting not that the
wings are destined for his own shoulders. "Behold," cried
his father, "the craft that shall bear us to our native land;
by its means we shall escape from Minos. Though Minos
may have closed all roads to us, he cannot close the highways
of the air. Cleave then the air, while still thou mayest, with
this my handiwork. But take heed thou draw not too nigh
the Virgin of Tegea, or to Orion, who, girt with his sword,
doth bear Boötes company. Shape thy course on mine. I
will lead the way; be content to follow me; with me to guide

thee, thou wilt have nought to fear. For, if in our airy
flight we soared too near the sun, the wax of our wings would
never bear the heat, and if we flew too low, the moisture of
the sea would weight our wings and make them over-heavy
for us to move. Fly then midway between; and O, my son,
beware the winds. Whithersoever they may blow, thither
let them waft thee." Thus he spake, and fitted the wings
upon his son's young shoulders and showed him how to move
them, even as the mother bird teaches her feeble fledglings
how to fly. That done, he fixes wings on to his own shoulders
and, half eager, half timid, launches himself on the un-
familiar track. Ere he begins his flight, he kisses his son,
and down the old man's cheeks the tears unbidden flow.

Not far from there, stands a hill, which, though less lofty
than a mountain, doth yet command the plain. It was from
there that they launched themselves on their perilous flight.
Dædalus, as he moves his own wings, gazes back at his son's,
yet nevertheless keeps steadily on his airy course. At first
the novelty of their flight enchants them; and ere long, casting all fear aside, Icarus grows more daring and essays a
bolder sweep. A fisherman, about to land a fish with his
slender rod, perceives them, and straightway lets it fall. Already they have left Samos behind on the left, and Naxos,
and Paros, and Delos dear to Apollo. On their right they
have Lebinthos, Calymna shaded with woods, and Astypalæa
girdled with pools where fish abound; when lo, young Icarus,
growing rash with boyish daring, steers a loftier course and
leaves his father. The bonds of his wings relax, the wax
melts as the sun grows near, and vainly he waves his arms,
they cannot catch the delicate air. Stricken with terror, he
looks down from the lofty heavens upon the sea beneath. A
darkness born of panic overspreads his eyes. And now the
wax has melted, he tosses his naked arms and quakes with
fear, for nought is there to upstay him. Down and down

he falls, and in his falling cries, "Father, O Father, all is over with me!" And the green waters sealed his mouth for ever. But the unhappy father—a father now no longer—cried, "Icarus, where art thou? Beneath what regions of the sky steerest thou thy flight? Icarus, Icarus," he cried and cried again, when lo, on the waste of waters he descried his wings. The land received the bones of Icarus; the sea retains his name.

Minos was powerless to stay a mortal's flight. I am essaying to hold a winged god. If any one deems there is any virtue in magic or in potions, he sadly errs. Neither the herbs of Medea nor the incantations of the Marsi will make love endure. If there were any potency in magic, Medea would have held the son of Æson, Circe would have held Ulysses. Philtres, too, that make the face grow pale, are useless when administered to women. They harm the brain and bring on madness. Away with such criminal devices! If you'd be loved, be worthy to be loved. Good looks and a good figure are not enough for that. Though you were Nireus, praised long ago by Homer; aye, were you young Hylas, snatched away by the guilty Naiads, if you would hold your mistress and not one day to be taken aback and find she's left you, add accomplishments of the mind to advantages of the person. Beauty is a fleeting boon; it fades with the passing years, and the longer it lives, the more surely it dies. The violets and wide-cupped lilies bloom not for ever, and, once the rose has blown, its naked stem shows only thorns. Thus, my fair youth, thy hair will soon grow white, and wrinkles soon will line thy face with furrows; so set thy beauty off with talents that shall mock at time; 'tis they alone will last unto the grave. Study the refinements of life, and enrich yourself with the treasures of the Greek and Latin tongues. Ulysses was not handsome, but he was eloquent, and two goddesses were tortured with love for him. How often Calypso groaned when she beheld him preparing to depart, and how she kept telling him that the waves would not suffer him to set sail. Times without number she asked him to tell her o'er again the story of the fall of Troy, times without number he would retell it in a new form. One day they were standing on the seashore: the fair nymph was begging him to tell her how the king of Thrace met his cruel death. Ulysses, with a twig which he chanced to have in his hand, drew her a plan upon the sand. "See, here is Troy," he said, tracing the line of the ramparts. "Here runs the Simois. Say this is my camp, farther along is the plain" (and he drew it) "which we stained with the blood of Dolon who tried to steal the horses of Achilles by night. There stood the tents of Rhesus, king of Thrace, and it was along there that I rode back with the horses that had been stolen from him." And so he was going on with his narrative, when suddenly a wave came and washed away Troy and Rhesus, together with his camp. Then said the goddess, "Seest thou what famous names these waves have swept away, and dost thou hope they will be kind to thee when thou settest sail?"

Well then, whoever you may be, put not too great a trust in the deceptive charm of beauty. Take care to possess something more than mere physical comeliness. What works wonders with the women is an ingratiating manner. Brusqueness and harsh words only promote dislike. We hate the hawk because it spends its life in fighting; and we hate the wolf that falls upon the timid flocks. But man snares not the swallow because it is gentle, and he suffers the dove to make its home in towers that he has built. Away with all strife and bitterness of speech. Pleasant words are the food of love. It is by quarrels that a woman estranges her husband, and a husband his wife. They imagine that in acting so they are paying each other out in their own coin. Leave them to it. Quarrels are the dowry which married folk bring one another. But a mistress should only hear agreeable things. It is not the law that has landed you in bed together. *Your* law, the law for you and her, is Love. Never approach her but with soft caresses and words that soothe her ear, so that she may always rejoice at your coming.

'Tis not to the rich that I would teach the art of Love. A man who can give presents has no need of any lessons I can teach him. He has wit enough, and to spare, if he can say when he pleases, "Accept this gift." I give him best. His means are mightier than mine. I am the poor man's poet; because I am poor myself and I have known what it is to be in love. Not being able to pay them in presents, I pay my mistresses in poetry. The poor man must be circumspect in his love-affairs; he mustn't permit himself to use strong language; he must put up with many things that a rich lover would never endure. Once I remember in a fit of ill-temper I ruffled my mistress's hair. It was a fit that robbed me of many and many a happy day. I did not notice that I had torn her dress, and I do not believe I had; but she said I had, and I was obliged to buy her another one. Good friends, be wiser than your master; don't do as he does, or, if you do, look out for squalls. Make war on the Parthians to your heart's content, but live at peace with your mistress; have recourse to playfulness and to whatever may excite love.

If your mistress is ungracious and off-hand in her manner towards you, bear it with patience; she'll soon come round. If you bend a branch carefully and gently, it won't break. If you tug at it suddenly with all your might, you'll snap it off. If you let yourself go with the stream, you'll get across the river in time, but if you try to swim against the tide, you'll never do it. Patience will soften tigers and Numidian lions; and slowly and surely you may accustom the bull to the rustic plow. What woman was ever more

tameless than Atalanta of Nonacris; yet, for all her arrogance, she yielded at length to a lover's tender assiduities. They say that many a time, beneath the trees, Milanion wept at his mishaps and at his mistress's unkindness. Often upon nis neck he bore, as he was bid, the treacherous toils; and often with his spear he pierced the savage boars. He was even struck by the arrows of Hylæus, but other darts, which were, alas, but too well known to him, had dealt him sorer wounds than that.

I do not bid thee climb, armed with thy bow, the woody heights of Mænalus, or carry heavy nets upon thy back. I do not bid thee bare thy breast to a foeman's arrows. If only thou art prudent, thou wilt find my precepts are not over-hard to carry out. If she's obstinate, let her have her way, and you'll get the better of her in the end. Only whatever she tells you to do, be sure you do it. Blame what she blames; like what she likes; say what she says; deny what she denies. If she smiles, smile too; if she sheds tears, shed them too. In a word, model your mood on hers. If she wants to play draughts, play badly on purpose and let her win the game. If you're playing dice, don't let her be piqued at losing, but make it look as though your luck was always out. If your battle-field's the chessboard, see to it that your men of glass are mown down by the foe.

Be sure and hold her parasol over her; and clear a way for her if she's hemmed in by the crowd; fetch a stool to help her on to the couch; and unlace or lace up the sandals on her dainty feet. And then, though you perish with cold yourself, you will often have to warm your mistress's icy hands in your bosom. And you mustn't mind, although it does seem a little undignified, holding up her mirror, like any slave, for her to look in. Why Hercules himself, who performed such mighty feats of bravery and strength, who won a seat in the Olympian realms he had carried on his shoulders, is said to have dwelt among the Ionian maids as one of them, to have held the work-basket and have spun coarse wool. The Tirynthian hero obeyed his mistress's commands; and will you hesitate to endure what he endured?

If your lady-love arranges to meet you in the Forum, be there well before the appointed time, and wait and wait till the very last minute. If she asks you to meet her somewhere else, leave everything and hurry off; don't let the crowd hinder you. If, at night, after she's been dining out, she calls a slave to see her home, be quick, offer your services. If you are in the country, and she writes saying, "Come at once," go to her, for Love brooks no delay. If you can't get a conveyance, then you must foot it. Nothing should stop you: thunder, heat, snow, nothing!

Love is like warfare. "Faint heart never won fair lady"; poltroons are useless in Love's service. The night, winter, long marches, cruel suffering, painful toil, all these things have to be borne by those who fight in Love's campaigns. Apollo, when he tended the herds of Admetus, dwelt, so 'tis said, in a humble cottage. Who would blush to do as Apollo did? If you would love long and well, you must put away pride. If the ordinary, safe route to your mistress is denied you, if her door is shut against you, climb up on to the roof and let yourself down by the chimney, or the skylight. How it will please her to know the risks you've run for her sake! 'Twill be an earnest of your love. Leander could often have done without his mistress, but he swam the strait to prove his courage.

Nor must you think it beneath your dignity to ingratiate yourself with her servants, even the humblest of them; greet each of them by name, and take their servile hands in yours. Give them (it will not cost you much) such presents as you can afford; and when the festival of Juno Caprotina comes round, make a handsome present to the lady's-maid. Get on

good terms with the occupants of the servants' hall, and don't
forget the porter or the slave that sleeps beside your lady's
door.

I don't advise you to make costly presents to your mistress;
offer her a few trifles, but let them be well chosen and appropriate to the occasion. When the country is displaying
all its lavish riches, and the branches of the trees are bending beneath their load, set some young slave to leave a basket
of fruit at her door. You can say they come from your place
in the country, though in reality you purchased them in
Rome. Send her grapes or chestnuts beloved of Amaryllis;
though the modern Amaryllis is no longer satisfied with
chestnuts. Or, again, a present of thrushes or pigeons will
prove that you have her still in mind. I know, of course,
that this same policy is followed by the expectant legatees
of some rich and childless dame. Out on such mean and
calculating generosity, say I! Shall I also advise you to send
poetry as well? Alas, verses don't count for much. Verses
come in for praise; but they really like gifts that are more
substantial than that. Even a barbarian, if only he is rich,
is sure to find favor. This is the golden age in very truth.
Gold will buy the highest honors; and gold will purchase
love. Homer himself, even if he came attended by the nine
Muses, would promptly be shown the door if he brought
no money to recommend him. Nevertheless, there *are* some
cultured women, but they are rare. There are others who
are not cultured but who wish to appear so. You must praise
them both in your poetry. Whatever the quality of your
lines, you may make them sound well if you know how to
read them with effect. Indeed, if the lines be well composed
and well delivered, the ladies will perhaps deign to regard
them as a trifling, a very trifling, present.

Now, when you have determined to do something that
you think will be of service, persuade your mistress to ask

you to do it. If you have made up your mind to free one of your slaves, see that he addresses his petition to her; if you've resolved not to punish another slave for some neglect of duty, see that it is she who gets the credit for this act of clemency. You'll get the benefit, she'll get the glory. You'll lose nothing, and she'll think she can twist you round her little finger.

If you want to keep your mistress's love, you must make her think you're dazzled with her charms. If she wears a dress of Tyrian purple, tell her there's nothing like Tyrian purple. If she's wearing a gown of Coan stuff, tell her that there's nothing becomes her so enchantingly. If she's ablaze with gold, tell her that you think gold's less brilliant than her charms. If she's clad in winter furs, tell her they're lovely; if she appears in a flimsy tunic, tell her she sets you on fire, and say you hope she won't catch cold. If she wears her hair parted on her forehead, say you like that style. If she has it frizzed and fuzzy, say, "How I love it frizzed!" Praise her arms when she dances, her voice when she sings, and when she ceases, say how sorry you are it came to an end so soon. If she admits you to her bed, adore the seat of all your bliss, and in tones trembling with delight tell her what a heaven she makes for you. Why, even if she were grimmer than the terrible Medusa, she would grow soft and docile for her love. Be a good dissembler and never let your face belie your words. Artifice is a fine thing when it's not perceived; once it's discovered, discomfiture follows. Confidence is gone for ever.

Often when the autumn is at hand, when the earth is adorned with all its charms, when the ruddy grape swells with its purple juice, when we feel alternately a nipping cold or an oppressive heat, this variation of temperature throws us into a state of languor. May your mistress then retain her health. But if some indisposition should compel

her to keep her bed, if she falls a victim to the evil effects
of the season, then is the time for you to show her how attentive and loving you can be; then is the time to sow the
seeds of the harvest you may gather later on. Be not deterred
by the attentions her malady demands. Render her whatever services she will deign to accept; let her behold you
shedding tears of compassion; never let her see you do not
want to kiss her, and let her parched lips be moistened with
your tears; say how you hope she'll soon be well again, and
be sure to let her hear you saying it, and always be prepared
to tell her you have had a dream of happy augury. Let some
old grandam, with trembling hands, come and sweeten her
bed and purify her room with sulphur and the expiatory
eggs. She will store up the memory of these kindnesses in
her heart. Many a time have people had legacies bequeathed
them for such trifling things as that. But be careful not
to display too much anxiety. Do not be over-busy. Your
affection and solicitude should have their limits. Don't make
it your business to restrict her diet, or tell her she mustn't
eat this or that. Don't bring her nasty medicine to drink;
leave all that to your rival.

But the wind to which you spread your sails when leaving
port is not the wind you need when you are sailing the open
sea. Love is delicate at birth; it becomes stronger with use.
Feed it with the proper food, and it will grow sturdy in
time. The bull that frightens you to-day, you used to stroke
when it was young. The tree that shelters you beneath its
shade was once but a frail sapling. A slender rivulet at its
source, the river gathers size little by little, and, as it flows,
is swollen with innumerable tributaries. See to it that thy
mistress grows accustomed to thee: nothing is so potent as
habit. To win her heart, let no trouble be too great. Let
her see you continually; let her hear none but you. Day and
night be present to her sight. But when you are sure that

she will long for you, then leave her alone, so that your absence may give her some anxiety. Let her repose awhile: the soil that is given a rest renders with usury the seed that's planted in it, and the ground that is parched greedily soaks in the water from the skies. As long as Phyllis had Demophoön at her side, her love for him was lukewarm. No sooner had he set sail, than she was consumed with passion for him. Ulysses, shrewd man, tortured Penelope by his absence, and with thy tears, Laodamia, didst thou yearn for the return of Protesilaus.

But be on the safe side; don't stay away too long; time softens the pangs of longing. Out of sight, out of mind. The absent lover is soon forgotten, and another takes his place. When Menelaus had departed, Helen grew weary of her lonely couch and sought warmth and consolation in the arms of her guest. Ah! Menelaus, what a fool wast thou! Alone didst thou depart, leaving thy wife beneath the same roof with a stranger. Fool, 'twas like delivering up the timid dove to the devouring kite, or surrendering the lamb to the hungry wolf. No, Helen was not to blame; her lover was not guilty; she was afraid to lie alone. Let Menelaus think what he will; Helen, in my view, was not to blame; all she did was to profit by her most accommodating husband.

But the fierce boar, in its wildest rage, when, making his last stand, he rolls the fleet hounds over and over; the lioness, when she offers her dugs to the cubs that she is suckling; the viper that the wayfarer has trodden upon with careless foot—all are less redoubtable than the woman who has caught another woman in her husband's bed. Her face is distorted with fury. The sword, the firebrand, anything that comes to her hand, she will seize. Casting all restraint aside, she will rush at her foe like a Mænad driven mad by the Aonian god. The barbarous Medea took vengeance on her own children for Jason's misdeeds and for his violation of the nuptial bond; that swallow that you see yonder was also an unnatural mother. See, her breast still bears the stain of blood. Thus do the happiest, the most firmly welded, unions fail. A cautious lover should beware of exciting these jealous furies.

Do not imagine that I am going to act the rigid moralist and condemn you to love but one mistress. The gods forbid. Even a married woman finds it difficult to keep such a vow as that. Take your fill of amusement, but cast the veil of modesty over your peccadilloes. Never make a parade of your good fortune, and never give a woman a present that another woman will recognize. Vary the time and place of your assignations, lest one of them catch you in some familiar place of rendezvous. When you write, be sure and read over what you have written; many women read into a letter much more than it is intended to convey.

Venus, when she is wounded, justly retaliates, gives the aggressor blow for blow and makes him feel, in his turn, the pain that he has caused. So long as Atrides was satisfied with his wife, she was faithful to him; her husband's infidelity drove her from the narrow path. She learned that Chryses, staff in hand and wearing the sacred fillet on his brows, had begged that his daughter should be restored to him, and begged in vain. She learned, O Briseis, of the abduction that pierced your heart with grief, and for what shameful reasons the war was dragging on. Still all this was only hearsay. But with her own eyes she had seen the daughter of Priam, she had, O sight of shame, seen the victor become the slave of his captive. From that day forth, the daughter of Tyndarus made Ægisthus free of her heart and bed, and took guilty vengeance for her husband's crime. Yet if, how well soever you may hide them, your secret amours come to light, never hesitate to deny your guilt. Be neither sheepish nor gushing, for these are sure signs of a guilty conscience.

But spare no effort and employ all your vigor in the battle of love. It's the only way to win peace; the only way to convince her of the unreality of her suspicions. Some people would advise you to stimulate your powers with noxious herbs, such as savory, pepper mixed with thistle-seed or yellow fever-few steeped in old wine. In my view these are nothing more nor less than poisons. The goddess, who dwells on the shady slopes of Mount Eryx, approves not such strained and violent means to the enjoyment of her pleasures. Nevertheless, you may take the white onion that comes from Megara and the stimulating plant that grows in our gardens, together with eggs, honey from Hymettus, and the apples of the lofty pine.

But wherefore, divine Erato, do we wander into these details of the Æsculapian art? Let my chariot return to its own particular track. Awhile ago I was counseling you to hide your infidelities: well, turn about, blazon abroad the conquests you have made. The curved ship is not always obedient to the same wind; she fleets o'er the waves, driven now by the North wind, now by the East. Turn by turn, the West wind and the South will fill her sails. Look at that driver on his chariot there. Sometimes he lets his reins hang loose, sometimes, with skillful hand, he restrains the ardor of his fiery steeds. There are lovers whom a hesitant indulgence ill-befriends. Their mistresses begin to languish if the apprehension of a rival comes not to stimulate their affections. Happiness will sometimes make us drunk and render difficult the way of constancy. A little fire will languish if it be not fed, and disappear beneath the gray ashes that accumulate upon it. But add a little sulphur, and lo, fresh flames will leap and sparkle with new splendor! Thus when the heart grows dull and torpid, apply, if you would wake it into life, the spur of jealousy. Give your mistress something to torment her, and bring new heat into her chilly heart. Let her grow pale at the evidence of your inconstancy. What happiness, what untold happiness is his, whose mistress's heart is wrung at the thought of her lover's infidelity. Soon she hears the tidings of his fault; while yet she is fain to hold the news untrue, she swoons and, hapless one, her cheeks grow pale as death, her lips refuse to speak. Oh, would I were that lover! I, whose hair she tears in her wild frenzy, whose face she fiercely scratches with her nails, at whose sight she bursts into floods of tears, but whom she will not, cannot live without! How long, you say, ought one to leave her in despair? Well, hasten to comfort her lest her wrath in the end should harden into bitterness. Hasten to fling thine arms about her snowy neck, and press her tear-stained cheek against thy breast. Kiss away her tears, and with her tears mingle the sweet delights of love. Soon she'll grow calm; that is the only way to soothe her wrath. When her rage is at its height, when 'tis open war between you, then beg her to ratify a peace upon her bed; she'll soon make friends. 'Tis there that, all unarmed, sweet concord dwells; 'tis there, the cradle of forgiveness. The doves that late were fighting, more tenderly will bill and coo; their murmurs seem to tell how true and tender is their love.

Nature, at first, was but a weltering chaos of sky and land and sea. But soon the heavens rose up above the earth, the sea encircled it with a liquid girdle; and from formless chaos issued forth the divers elements. The woods were peopled with wild things, the air with light-wingèd birds; and the fishes hid themselves beneath the deep waters. In those times men wandered lonely over the face of the earth, and brute strength was their sole resource. The forest was their dwelling-place, the grass their food, dry leaves their bed, and for a long time each man dwelt in ignorance of his fellows. Then came the sweet delights of love, and softened, so they say, these rugged hearts, bringing together man and woman on a single couch. No tutor did they need to tell them what to do; Venus, without recourse to any art, fulfilled her gentle office. The bird has his beloved mate; the fish beneath the waters finds another fish to share his pleasure; the hind follows the stag; the snake mates with the snake; the dog with the bitch; the ewe and the heifer yield themselves with delight to the caresses of the ram and the bull; the goat, noisome though he be, repels not the caresses of his lascivious fellow; the mare, burning with the frenzy of desire, will speed o'er hill and dale, and even through rivers, to join her stallion. Be of good cheer then and employ this potent remedy to calm the anger of thy mistress; 'tis the only sovran cure for her aching sorrow; 'tis a balm sweeter than the juices of Machaon, and if you happen to have erred a little, it will surely bring you pardon.

Such was the burden of my song, when on a sudden Apollo appeared to me and touched with his fingers the chords of a golden lyre; in his hand he bore a branch of laurel; a laurel wreath encircled his brow. Prophetic was his mien and prophetic the voice with which he bade me lead my disciples into his temple. "There," said he, "you will find this inscription famous throughout the whole world, 'Man, know thyself.' The man who knows himself follows ever in his love-affairs the precepts of wisdom. He alone hath wit to adapt his enterprises to his powers. If he is endowed with comely looks, if he has a beautiful skin, let him lie, when he is in bed, with his shoulders uncovered; if he is an attractive talker, let him not maintain a glum silence. If he can sing, let him sing; if the wine makes him merry, let him drink. But whatever he is, orator, babbler, or fine frenzied poet, don't let him interrupt the conversation in order to declaim his prose or his verse." Thus spake Phœbus, and, lovers, you will do well to obey him; nought but the truth ever issued from his god-like lips.

But, to my subject. Whosoever loves wisely and follows the precepts of my art is sure to conquer and to attain the object of his heart's desire. The furrows do not always repay with interest the seed that has been sown therein; the winds do not always waft the bark on its uncertain course. Few pleasures, many pains—such is the lot of lovers. Harsh are the trials which they must expect to face. As numerous as the hares on Athos, as the bees on Hybla, as the olives on the tree of Pallas, as the shells upon the seashore, are the sorrows that Love engenders. The arrows he aims at us are steeped in gall. Perhaps they will tell you that your mistress is out, when you know very well she's in, because you've seen her. Never mind, make believe she is out and that your eyes have deceived you. She has promised to let you in at night, and you find her door shut; be patient and lie down on the cold damp ground. Peradventure, some lying servant will come, and looking at you with an insolent stare, say, "What does this fellow want, always besieging our door like this?" Then you must turn the other cheek to this grim seneschal and speak him fair, and not him only, but the door as well, and on the threshold lay the roses that adorned your brow. If your mistress gives you leave, haste to her side; if she will none of you, withdraw. A well-bred man ought never to make himself a burden. Would you compel her to exclaim, "Is there no way of getting rid of this pestilent fellow?" Women often take unreasonable whims into their head. Never mind; put up with all her insults; never mind if she kicks you even; kiss her dainty feet.

But why linger over such minor details? Let us turn to more important themes. I am going to sing of lofty things. Ye lovers all, lend me your ears. My enterprise is fraught with danger; but without danger, where would courage be? The object I aim at is not easy of attainment. If you have a rival, put up with him without a murmur, and your triumph is assured. You will mount, a conqueror, to Jove's high temple. Believe me, these are not the words of a mere mortal. They are oracles as sure as any that Dodona ever gave. This is the very climax of the art that I impart. If your mistress exchanges meeting glances with your rival— nods and becks and wreathèd smiles—put up with it. If she writes him letters, never scrutinize her tablets; let her come and go as she pleases. Hosts of husbands show this indulgence to their lawful wives, especially when thou, soft slumber, aidest in the deceit. Nevertheless, I confess that, in my own case, I cannot attain this degree of perfection. What am I to do? I cannot rise to the height of my own precepts. If I saw a rival making signs to my mistress before my very eyes, do you think I should put up with it, and not give free rein to my wrath? I remember one day her husband kissed her. How I raved and swore about it! Love is made up of these unreasonable demands. This shortcoming has often been my undoing where women are concerned. It is much cleverer of a man to let others have the entrée to his mistress. The really proper course is not to know anything about it. Suffer her to hide her infidelities, lest forcing her to confess them should teach her to control her blushes. Ye youthful lovers, then, take heed not to catch your mistresses in the act, lest, while deceiving you they should imagine you were taken in by their fine speeches. Two lovers, who have been found out, do but love each other the more ardently. When they share a common lot, they both persist in the conduct that brought about their undoing.

There is a story well known throughout Olympus: 'tis the story of Mars and Venus caught in the act by Vulcan's cunning ruses. Mars, having fallen madly in love with Venus, changed from the grim warrior to the submissive lover. Venus (and never was there a goddess with a heart more tender), Venus showed herself neither awkward nor unfeeling. How many and many a time, they say, the wanton woman laughed at her husband's shambling gait, and at his hands made horny by the heat of the forge and by hard toil. How charming Mars thought her when she imitated the old blacksmith, and how her graceful motions set off her loveliness. To begin with they took the utmost care to conceal their intrigue, and their guilty passion was full of modesty and reserve. But the Sun (nothing ever eludes his glance), the Sun revealed to Vulcan the conduct of his spouse. Ah, Old Sol, what a bad example you set! Demand the favors of the goddess; make her acquiescence the price of your silence; she has the wherewithal to pay you. All around and about his bed Vulcan cunningly stretches a network invisible to every eye. Then he pretends to set out for Lemnos. The two lovers hie them to the familiar spot, and both of them, naked as Cupid himself, are enveloped in the traitorous toils. Then Vulcan calls on the gods to gather round and bids them gaze upon the imprisoned lovers. Venus, so 'tis said, could scarce keep from weeping. They could not hide their faces in their hands, nor cover their nakedness. One of the onlookers thus spoke jeeringly to Mars: "Valiant Mars," quoth he, "if thy chains are too heavy for thee, hand them on to me." At length, yielding to the prayers of Neptune, Vulcan set the two captives free. Mars withdrew to Thrace; Venus to Paphos. Say now, Vulcan, what didst thou gain thereby? Erstwhile they hid their loves; now they freely and openly indulge their passion; they have banished all shame. You'll soon be sorry that you were such a prying fool! Indeed they say that even now you regret that you ever gave way to your anger.

No traps! I forbid you to use them; and Venus herself, who was caught by her spouse, forbids you to make use of tricks, whereof she was the victim. Don't go laying snares for your rival. Don't try and intercept love-letters. Leave such devices, if they think it well to employ them, to lawful husbands whose rights are hallowed by sacred fire and water. As for me, I proclaim it yet again, I only sing of pleasures which the law permits.

Who would dare divulge to the profane the mysteries of Ceres and the pious rites instituted in Samothrace? It redounds but little to our credit to keep silence when we are commanded so to do; but to blurt out things we ought to know should be kept secret is a most grievous thing. Rightly was Tantalus punished for his indiscretion, rightly was he debarred from reaching the fruits that hung above his head; it served him right that he should parch with thirst with water all around him. Cytherea, especially, forbids that her mysteries should be revealed. I give thee warning, no babbling knaves should ever draw near her altars. If the sacred emblems of her worship are not concealed in mystic baskets; if no brazen cymbals are beaten at her festivals; if she opens the doors of her temple to all, it is on condition that none shall divulge her mysteries. Venus herself never putteth off her veil, but with modest hand she covereth her charms. The beasts of the field abandon themselves, in any place and in the sight of all, to the delights of love, and often at the spectacle a young girl will turn away her head; but for our loves we must have a secret bower, closed doors, and we must needs cover with vesture the secret places of our body. Even if we seek not for darkness, we like a certain dimness, at all events something a little less than broad daylight. Thus when men and women still went unprotected against the sun and the rain, when the oak provided them with food and shelter, 'twas not in the open, but in caves and woods, that they enjoyed the sweet pleasures of love, so great was the respect which mankind, though still uncouth, entertained for the laws of modesty. Now we make a parade of our nocturnal exploits, and people, it seems, would pay a high

price for the pleasure of divulging them. Nay, isn't it the
fashion nowadays to stop and talk to a girl everywhere one
goes, so as to be able to say, "You saw that girl, she's another one I've had!" It's all because they want to have some
one to point at; so that every woman who is the object of
these attentions becomes the talk of the town. But there's
nothing really in it. There are men who invent stories which,
if they were true, they would repudiate. To hear them talk,
you would think that no woman ever resisted them. If they
can't touch their person, they at least attack their good name,
and though their body be chaste, their reputation is tarnished.
Go, thou hateful warder, and shut the doors upon thy mistress; bolt her in with a hundred bolts. What avail such
precautions against the slanderer who brags with lying tongue
of the favors he has failed to obtain? Let us, on the other
hand, speak sparingly of our real amours, and hide our secret
pleasures beneath an impenetrable veil.

Never speak to a woman about her defects; many a lover
has had occasion to congratulate himself on having observed
this very profitable reticence. The wingèd-footed hero, Perseus, never found fault with Andromeda for her swarthy
skin. Andromache was, in every one's opinion, far too tall;
Hector was the only one who considered her of the average
height. Accustom yourself to the things you don't like;
you'll learn to put up with them; habit makes a lot of things
acceptable. At first, Love will be put off by the merest
trifle. A freshly-grafted branch that is just beginning to
draw the sap from the green bark will fall off if the slightest
breath of wind disturbs it; but if you give it time to grow
strong, it will soon resist the winds and, developing into a
sturdy branch, enrich the tree that bears it with its alien
fruit. Time effaces everything, even bodily defects, and
what we once looked upon as blemishes will one day cease
to seem so. At first, our nostrils cannot bear the smell of

the hides of bulls; they grow used to it in time and bear it without distress.

Moreover, there are words you can employ to palliate defects. If a woman's skin is blacker than Illyrian pitch, tell her she's a brunette. If she squints a little, tell her she's like Venus. If she's carroty, tell her she's like Minerva. If she's so skinny you would think she was at death's door, tell her she has a graceful figure. If she's short, so much the better, she's all the lighter. If she's thick-waisted, why she's just agreeably plump. Similarly, you must disguise every defect under the name of its nearest quality. Never ask her how old she is, or who was consul when she was born. Leave it to the Censor to perform that uncomfortable duty, especially if she has passed the flower of her youth, if the summer of her days is over, and if she is already compelled to pull out her gray hairs. My young friends, that age, and even an older one than that, is not without its pleasures. It is a field that you should sow and one day you will reap your harvest. Labor while your strength and your youth allow. All too soon tottering eld, with noiseless tread, will be upon you. Cleave the waters of the ocean with your oar, or the glebe with your plow; wield with warlike arm the deadly sword, or devote to women your vigor and your care. 'Tis but another kind of military service, and in it, too, rich trophies may be won.

Nor should it be forgotten that women, who are getting on in years, have experience, and it is only experience that sets the seal of perfection on our natural gifts. They repair by their toilet the ravages of time, and by the care they take of themselves manage to conceal their age. They know all the different attitudes of Love and will assume them at your pleasure. No pictured representation can rival them in voluptuousness. With them pleasure comes naturally, without provocation, the pleasure which is sweeter than all, the pleas-

ure which is shared equally by the man and the woman. I
hate those embraces in which both do not consummate; that
is why boys please me but little. I hate a woman who offers
herself because she ought to do so, and, cold and dry, thinks
of her sewing when she's making love. The pleasure that
is granted to me from a sense of duty ceases to be a pleasure
at all. I won't have any woman doing her duty towards
me. How sweet it is to hear her voice quaver as she tells
me the joy she feels, and to hear her imploring me to slacken
my speed so as to prolong her bliss. How I love to see her,
drunk with delight, gazing with swooning eyes upon me, or,
languishing with love, keeping me a long while at arm's
length.

But these accomplishments are not vouchsafed by nature
to young girls. They are reserved for women who have
passed the age of thirty-five. Let who will hasten to drink
new and immature wine. Let me have a rich mellow vintage
dating back to one of our elder consuls. It is only after
many years that the plane tree affords a shelter from the
scorching sun, and fields but newly reaped hurt the naked
foot. What! do you mean to tell me you would put Hermione before Helen? And would Althaea's daughter out-
rival her mother? If you would enjoy the fruits of love in
their maturity, you will obtain, if only you persevere, a reward worthy of your desires.

But already the bed, the minister of their pleasures, has
received our two lovers. Stay thy steps, my Muse, at the
closed door. They will know well enough, without thy aid,
what words to say to one another, and their hands within the
bed will not be idle. Their fingers will find the way to those
secret places in which Love is wont to proclaim his presence.
'Twas even thus that the valiant Hector, whose skill was not
confined to battle, bore himself with Andromache. Thus
too the great Achilles fondled his fair captive when, weary

of fighting, he lay beside her on the downy couch. Thou didst not fear, Briseis, to yield thyself to the caresses of those hands that bore upon them still the stains of Trojan blood. Was there aught to compare, voluptuous girl, with the pleasure of feeling the pressure of those victorious hands?

If you listen to my advice, you will not be in too great a hurry to attain the limits of your pleasure. Learn, by skillful dallying, to reach the goal by gentle, pleasant stages. When you have found the sanctuary of bliss, let no foolish modesty arrest your hand. Then will you see the love-light trembling in her eyes, even as the rays of the sun sparkle on the dancing waves. Then will follow gentle moanings mingled with murmurings of love, soft groans and sighs and whispered words that sting and lash desire. But now beware! Take heed lest, cramming on too much sail, you speed too swiftly for your mistress. Nor should you suffer her to outstrip you. Speed on together towards the promised haven. The height of bliss is reached when, unable any longer to withstand the wave of pleasure, lover and mistress at one and the same moment are overcome. Such should be thy rule when time is yours and fear does not compel you to hasten your stolen pleasures. Nevertheless, if there be danger in delay, lean well forward, and drive your spur deep into your courser's side.

My task draws toward its end. Young lovers, show your gratitude. Give me the palm and wreathe my brow with the fragrant myrtle. As Podalirius was famous among the Greeks for his skill in curing disease, Pyrrhus for his valor, Nestor for his eloquence; as Calchas was famed for his skill in foretelling the future, Telamon for wielding weapons, Automedon for chariot-racing, so do I excel in the art of Love. Lovers, laud your poet, sing my praises, so that my name may resound throughout the world. I have given you arms. Vulcan gave arms to Achilles. With them he was victorious. Learn ye too to conquer with mine. And let every lover, who shall have triumphed over a doughty Amazon with the sword I gave him, inscribe on his trophies, "Ovid was my Master."

But now the girls, look you, want me to give them some lessons. You, my dears, shall be my instant care.

THE ART OF LOVE

BOOK III

I HAVE just armed the Greeks against the Amazons; now, Penthesilea, it remains for me to arm thee against the Greeks, thee and thy valiant troop. Fight with equal resources and let the victory go to the side favored by beloved Dione and the boy who flies over the whole world. It was not right to expose you, all defenseless as you were, to the attacks of a well-armed foe. Victory, my men, at such a price as that would be a disgrace.

But perchance one among you will say to me, "Wherefore give fresh poison to the snake, wherefore surrender the lamb to the raging wolf?" Now forbear to condemn the whole sex for the crimes of a few of its members; let every woman be judged on her own merits. If the young Alcides had reason to complain of Helen, if his elder brother could with justice accuse Clytemnestra, Helen's sister; if, through the crime of Eriphyle, the daughter of Talaos, Amphiaraus went riding to the under-world on his living steeds, is it not also true that Penelope remained chaste when sundered from her husband who was kept for ten years fighting before Troy and who, when Troy had fallen, wandered over the seas for ten years more? Look at Laodamia, who, in order to join her husband in the grave, died long before her tale of years was told. And Alcestis, who, by sacrificing her own life, redeemed her husband, Admetus, from the tomb. "Take me in thine arms, Capaneus, and let our ashes at least be mingled," exclaimed the daughter of Iphis, and forthwith leapt into the midst of the pyre.

Virtue is a woman both in vesture and in name; what wonder, therefore, that she should favor her own sex? Nevertheless, it is not these lofty souls that my art requires; lighter sails are suited to my pinnace. Only wanton loves are the burden of my discourse; to women I am about to teach the art of making themselves beloved.

Woman cannot resist the flames and cruel darts of love, shafts which, methinks, pierce not the heart of man so deeply. Man is ever a deceiver; woman deceives but rarely. Make a study of women, you'll find but few unfaithful ones among them. False Jason cast off Medea when she was already a mother, and took another woman to his arms. It is no thanks to thee, O Theseus, that Ariadne, abandoned on an unknown shore, fell not a prey to the birds of the sea.

Wherefore did Phyllis return nine times to the seashore? Ask that question of the woods, who, in sorrow for her loss, shed their green raiment. Thy guest, Dido, for all his much-belauded conscience, fled from thee leaving thee nought save the sword that brought thee death. Ah, hapless ones, shall I reveal to you the cause of your undoing? You knew not how to love. You lacked the art, and art makes love endure. And even now they would still continue in their ignorance, but that Cytherea bids me instruct them. Into my presence did Cytherea come and thus she did command. "What ill, then, have they wrought thee, these unhappy women, that thou deliverest them, all defenseless as they are, into the hands of the men whom thou thyself hast armed? Thou hast devoted two poems to instructing men. And now the women in their turn demand thy aid. The poet who had outpoured the vials of his scorn on the wife of Menelaus, soon repented, and sang her praises in a palinode. If I know thee truly, thou art not the man to be unkind to the women. Thou wouldst rather seek to serve them so long as thou dost live." Thus she spake, and from the wreath that crowned her hair, she took a leaf and a few myrtle berries, the which she gave to me. As I took them, an influence divine was shed about me. The air shone purer round about me, and it seemed as though a burden had been lifted from my heart.

While Venus inspires me, my fair ones, give ear unto my counsel. Modesty and the law and your privileges permit. Bethink you, then, of old age which cometh all too soon, and not an instant will you lose. While yet you may, and while you yet enjoy the spring-time of your years, taste of the sweets of life. The years flow on like to the waters of a river. The stream that fleeteth by, never returns to the source whence it sprang. The hour that hath sped returns again no more. Make the most of your youth; youth that flies apace. Each new day that dawns is less sweet than those which went before. Here, where the land is rough with withering bracken, I have seen the violet bloom; from this thorny bush, I once did wreathe me garlands of roses. Thou who rejectest love, to-day art but a girl; but the time will come when, all alone and old, thou wilt shiver with cold through the long dark hours in thy solitary bed. No more shall rival swains come of a night and, battling for your favors, batter down your doors; no more, of a morning, will you find your threshold strewn with roses. Ah me! How soon the wrinkles come; how swiftly fades the color from the beauteous cheek! Those white hairs, which (so at least you swear) you had when you were quite a child, will swiftly cover all your head. The snake, when he sloughs off his skin, sloughs off the burden of his years, and the stag, when he sprouts new horns, renews his youth. But nothing brings amends for what Time filches from us. Pluck, then, the rose and lose no time, since if thou pluck it not 'twill fall forlorn and withered, of its own accord. Besides, the toil of child-bearing shortens the span of youth; too frequent harvests make the soil wax old. Blush not, O Phœbe, that thou didst love Endymion upon the Latmian height. And Dawn, thou goddess of the rosy fingers, that thou didst bear off Cephalus, was no shame to thee. Nay, though of Adonis we refrain to speak, whom Venus still doth mourn to-day, to whom, if not to love, owed she Æneas and Hermione? Follow then, ye mortal maidens, in the footsteps of these goddesses; withhold not your favors from your ardent lovers.

If they deceive you, wherein is your loss? All your charms remain; and even if a thousand should partake of them, those charms would still be unimpaired. Iron and stone will wear thin by rubbing; that precious part of you defies attrition, and you need never fear 'twill wear away. Doth a torch lose aught of its brightness by giving flame to another torch? Should we fear to take water from the mighty ocean? "A woman," you will say, "ought not thus to give herself to a man." Come now, why not? What does she lose? Nought but the liquid which she may take in again at will. Ah, no! I am not telling you to make drabs of yourselves; but merely not to be scared of some imaginary ill; the bestowal of such gifts will never make you poor.

But I am still within the harbor. A gentle breeze will waft me to the main. Once well out on the open sea, I shall be borne along by a stronger wind. Let me begin with dress. A well-tended vine yields a good harvest, and high stands the corn on the well-tilled field. Good looks are the gift of God; but how few can pride themselves upon their beauty. The majority of you have not been vouchsafed this favor. A careful toilet will make you attractive, but without such attention, the loveliest faces lose their charm, even were they comparable to those of the Idalian goddess herself. If the beautiful women of ancient times recked not of their appearance, the men were not a whit less careless. If Andromache arrayed herself in a coarse tunic, why should we marvel? She was the wife of a rugged soldier. Would the wife of Ajax come richly appareled to a warrior clad in the hides of seven oxen? In those far-off days, the ways of our forefathers were rude and simple. Rome nowadays is all ablaze with gold, rich with the wealth of the world that she hath conquered. Look at the Capitol; compare it now with what it once was. You would say it was a temple consecrated to another Jupiter. The palace of the Senate, worthy now of the august assembly that sits within it, was, in the days when Tatius was king, nothing but a thatched cottage. These gorgeous edifices on the Palatine Hill, built in honor of Apollo and our great leaders, were once but pasture ground for oxen that dragged the plow. Let others belaud those ancient times; I am satisfied to be a child of to-day. I find it better suited to my taste, not because nowadays we ransack the bowels of the earth for gold, and import purple dyes from distant shores; not because we see the mountains shrink because we are eternally quarrying them for marble; not because vast moles keep far away the billows of the deep; but because we enjoy the amenities of life, and because those rough and boorish ways, which for a long time characterized our ancestors, have not endured to our day.

Nevertheless, burden not your ears with those sumptuous pearls which the dusky Indian seeks beneath the green waves. Go not forth in garments heavily inwrought with gold. The wealth by which you would fain attract us, very often just repels us. Neatness is what we like. Let your hair be nicely done. That depends greatly on the skill of the person that dresses it. Of course there are innumerable ways of doing it. Every woman should study to find out the style that suits her best; and for that her mirror is the surest guide! Long features demand that the hair should be simply parted on the forehead. Such was the style of Laodamia. Women with round faces should wear their hair lightly twisted into a knot on the top of the head, leaving the ears exposed. One woman will let her hair fall loose on either shoulder, like Apollo when he holds his dulcet lyre. Another must needs have her hair tied up behind, like Diana when she pursueth the wild beasts in the forests. One delights us with her loose

flowing ringlets, another by wearing her hair closely patted
down upon her temples. Some women like to adorn their
hair with the shell of the Cyllenian tortoise, others to wear
it in towering waves. But there are not more acorns on an
oak tree, more bees on Hybla, or wild beasts on the mountains, than there are modes of doing a woman's hair, and
new ones are invented every day. Some women look well
with their hair done in careless fashion: you might think it
hadn't been done since yesterday. In point of fact it has
only just been combed. Artifice should look like careless-
ness. Such was Iole when Hercules first saw her in the captured city. "That is the woman for me," he exclaimed.
Such, too, was Ariadne, forsaken on the shores of Naxos,
when Bacchus bore her away in his chariot, while the Satyrs
cried, "Evoë." Ah, you women! Nature, kindly toward
your charms, has given you how many means to repair the
ravages of time! We men, alas, grow bald. Our hair, of
which time robs us, falls even as the leaves when the North
wind brings them down. A woman will dye her hair with
the juice of some German herb; and the artificial color becomes her better than the natural one. A woman will appear
wearing a mass of hair that she has just purchased. For a
little money she can buy another's tresses. She'll do the deal
without a blush, quite openly, in front of Hercules and the
Virgin band.

Now what shall I say about clothes? I care not for those
golden flounces, or wool twice dipped in Tyrian purple?
There are so many other colors that cost less money. Why
carry all your fortune on your back? Look at this azure
blue like a clear sky when the wind has ceased to herd the
rain clouds from the South. Now look, too, at this golden
yellow; 'tis the color of the ram which once on a time saved
Phryxus and Helle from the snares of Ino. That green is
called water-green from the color that it imitates; I could

easily imagine that the Nymphs were clothed in such apparel. This hue resembles saffron; it is the color wherein Aurora arrays herself when, moist with dew, she yokes her shining coursers to her car. There you will recognize the color of the myrtle of Paphos; here the purple amethyst, the whitening rose, or the Thracian stork; and here again the color of thy chestnuts, Amaryllis, or thy almonds, or the color of that stuff to which wax has given its name. As numerous as the flowers which blow when sluggish Winter hath departed, and when beneath the Spring's soft breath, the vine puts forth its buds, so many and more are the hues that wool receives from all its many dyes. Choose then with care, for all colors are not becoming to all people. Black suits a fair complexion: it became Briseis; she was dressed in black when she was carried off. White suits dark people; white, Andromeda, set off your charms, and 'twas white that you were wearing when you set foot on the isle of Seriphos.

I was going to tell you not to let your armpits smell, and to see that your legs were not rough with bristles. But it's not, of course, to the coarse Caucasian women I am addressing my remarks, nor yet to the women who drink the waters of the Caicus. I need not tell you never to neglect to keep your teeth white and to rinse your mouth out every morning with clean water. With wax you know how to whiten your skin, and with carmine to give yourself the rosy hue which Nature has denied you. Your art will tell you how to fill the space between your eyebrows, if it be too faintly marked, and how, with cosmetics, to conceal the all too patent evidence of the growing years. You fear not to increase the brightness of your eyes with finely powdered ash, or with the saffron that grows on the banks of the Cydnus. I have told of the ways of restoring beauty in a work, which though slender, is of great value by reason of the studied care with which I wrote it. Consult it for the remedies you

need, all you young women on whom Nature has not lavished her favors. You will find my treatise abounds in useful
counsel.

But on no account let your lover find you with a lot of
"aids to beauty" boxes about you. The art that adorns you
should be unsuspected. Who but would feel a sensation of
disgust if the paint on your face were so thick that it oozed
down on to your breasts? What words could describe the
sickening smell of the œsypum although it comes from
Athens; that oily juice which they extract from the fleece
of sheep. I should also disapprove of your using stag's marrow, or of your cleaning your teeth when any one is there
to see. I know all that would enhance your charms, but the
sight would be none the less disagreeable. How many things
revolt us in the process, which delight us in the achievement.
Those famous masterpieces of the sculptor Myron were once
but useless, shapeless blocks of marble. If you want a ring
of gold, you've got to hammer it into shape; the material
you wear was once dirty, evil-smelling wool. That marble,
once an unhewn block, is now a masterpiece—Venus, naked,
wringing the water from her dripping hair. Let your servants tell us you are still asleep, if we arrive before your
toilet's finished. You will appear all the lovelier when you've
put on the finishing touch. Why should I know what it is
that makes your skin so white? Keep your door shut, and
don't let me see the work before it's finished. There are a
whole host of things we men should know nothing about.
Most of these various artifices would give us a nasty turn,
if you didn't take care not to let us see them. Look at
those brilliant ornaments that adorn the stage. If you ex-
amined them closely, you would see that they are merely
gilded wood. None of the audience are allowed to go near
till everything is finished and in order. Just in the same way,

it's only when the men are away that you ought to do your titivating.

Howbeit, I do not by any means forbid you to comb your hair before us; I love to see it fall in floating tresses about your shoulders. But never get vexed or petulant, and don't keep on fidgeting with your curls. Don't treat your maid so as to make her in terror of you. I detest the sort of shrew that scratches her maid's face, or sticks a needle in her arm, in a fit of temper. It makes the poor girl wish the devil would take the head she is holding between her hands, and with blood and tears she moistens her mistress's hateful tresses. Every woman who has but little hair should have a sentinel at her door, or else always have her hair attended to in the temple of the Bona Dea. One day I was announced unexpectedly to my mistress, and in her flurry she put on her false hair all awry. May such a mischance never befall any but our enemies! May such a disgrace be reserved for the daughters of the Parthians. A mutilated animal, a barren field, a leafless tree are hideous things to see: a bald head is not less so.

'Tis not to you, Semele or Leda, that I address my lessons, nor to thee, O fair Sidonian, who wast borne by a fictitious bull across the seas; nor yet to Helen whom thou with reason, Menelaus, didst demand, and whom thou, her ravisher, did with equal reason refuse to give up. My host of pupils is composed of fair women and of plain, and these latter always outnumber the rest. The pretty ones are less in need of art's assistance and take its admonitions less to heart; they are the fortunate possessors of charms whose potency owes nought to art. When the sea is calm, the mariner lays him down to rest in careless ease; when the tempest sets it on a roar, he quits not his station even for an instant.

Rare, however, is the face without a fault. Hide these blemishes with care, and so far as may be, conceal the defects

of your figure. If you are short, sit down, lest when standing you should be thought to be sitting; if you are a dwarf,
lie stretched at full length on your couch, and so that none
may see how short you are, throw something over your feet
to hide them. If you are thin, wear dresses of thick material
and have a mantle hanging loosely about your shoulders. If
you are sallow, put on a little rouge; if you are swarthy, see
what the fish of Pharos will do for you. Let an ungainly
foot be hid in a white leathern shoe. If your legs are thin,
don't be seen unlacing your sandals. If your shoulder-blades
are prominent, little pads will correct the defect. If you
have too full a bust, contain it with a *brassière*. If your
fingers are stumpy and your nails unsightly, don't gesticulate
when you are talking. If your breath is strong, you should
never talk when your stomach's empty, and always keep
some distance away from your lover. A woman whose teeth
are discolored, or prominent, or uneven, will often give herself away when she laughs. Who would imagine it? Women
are even taught how to laugh. Even in such a detail as that,
they study to be charming. Don't open your mouth too
wide; let the dimples on either side be small, and let the
extremity of the lips cover the upper part of the teeth.
Don't laugh too often and too loud. Let there be something feminine and gentle in your laughter, something agreeable to the ear. Some women cannot laugh without making
a hideous grimace; others try to show how pleased they are,
and you would imagine they were crying; others offend the
ear with harsh and ugly sounds; like the noise a dirty old
she-ass makes as she brays at the mill-stone.

Where indeed does Art not have a say! Why, women even
learn to weep gracefully; to cry when they will, and as much
as they will. And then there are women who don't pronounce a certain letter in their words and lisp with affectation when they come to it. This assumed defect lends them

an added charm; so they actually practice speaking imperfectly. All these are details, but, since they have their uses, practice them assiduously. Learn also how to walk as a woman should. There is a style in walking that should be carefully cultivated; and that style, or the lack of it, will often attract or repel a stranger. This woman, for example, walks with an elegant swing from the hips; her gown floats gracefully in the breeze, and she moves with dignity and charm. And here again is a woman who elbows her way along with huge strides like the red-faced wife of an Umbrian peasant. But in this matter of walking, as in everything else, we must have a sense of proportion. One woman will walk too much like a country wench, another with overmuch mincing and affectation. Then, again, you should leave uncovered the top of your shoulder and the upper part of your left arm. That is especially becoming to women who have a white skin. At the mere sight of it, I should be mad to cover all I could touch with kisses.

The Sirens were monsters of the deep, and, with their wondrous singing, stayed the swiftest vessels in their flight. When their song fell upon his ears, Ulysses was sore tempted to unbind himself from the mast; as for his companions, their ears were stopped with wax. Music is a soothing thing. Women should learn to sing. Many a woman has made up for her lack of beauty by the sweetness of her voice. Sometimes sing over the songs you have heard at the theater; sometimes sing voluptuous, Oriental airs. A woman, who is fain to attract, should know how to play the lute and the harp. Thracian Orpheus, with his lyre, charmed rocks and wild beasts, aye, and Acheron and the triple-headed Cerberus. And thou, Amphion, righteous avenger of thy mother's wrong, didst thou not behold stones rise up at the sound of thy voice and range themselves into walls? Who has not heard of the wonders wrought by Arion with his lyre? Even the dumb fish is said to have listened, enchanted, to his song. Learn, too, to sweep the strings of the joyous psaltery with either hand. 'Tis an instrument favorable to the dalliance of lovers. You should also learn Callimachus by heart, and Philetas and Anacreon, who loved his drop of wine. And Sappho too; for what is more exciting than her verse? Then there's the poet who tells us about a father being hoodwinked by the crafty Geta. You might also read the verses of the tender-souled Propertius, and the poems of my beloved Tibullus, and something out of Gallus, or the poem Varro wrote about the golden fleece so bitterly lamented, Phrixus, by thy sister; and the story of the fugitive Æneas, and the origins of lofty Rome; for Latium boasts no prouder masterpiece than that. And peradventure shall my name with theirs be numbered, and my writings shall not be given over to the waters of Lethe, and perchance some one will say, "Read o'er these dainty lines wherein our Master gives instruction both to men and women; or choose, in those three books, the which he calls the Loves, passages which you will read with sweetly modulated voice; or, if thou wilt, declaim with skill one of those letters from his Heroines, a kind of work unknown before his time and whereof he himself was the inventor." Hear my prayers, O Phœbus, hear them, mighty Bacchus, and you, ye Muses, divine protectresses of poets.

Who could doubt that I want my charmer to be skilled in the dance? I would that, when the wine-cup is placed upon the table, she should be accomplished in swaying her arms to the measure of the music. Graceful dancers delight your theater-goer. Such grace, such airy lightness, charms us all.

I am loth to enter into petty details, but I should like my pupil to know how to throw the dice with skill, and to calculate with nicety the impetus she gives them as she tosses them on to the table. I should like her to know when to throw the three numbers, and when to take and when to call. I should wish her to play chess with skill and caution. One piece against two is bound to go under. A king that is battling, separated from his queen, is liable to be taken; and his rival is often compelled to retrace his steps. Again, when the ball bounces against the broad racquet, you must only touch the one you intend to serve. There is another game divided into as many parts as there are months in the year. A table has three pieces on either side; the winner must get all the pieces in a straight line. It is a bad thing for a woman not to know how to play, for love often comes into being during play.

Still, it is only half the battle merely to play well; the important thing is to be master of yourself. Sometimes, when we are not properly on our guard, when we are carried away by the heat of the game, we forget ourselves and let our inmost nature stand revealed. Rage and love of gain, such are the shameful vices that lay hold on us; thence spring quarrels, brawls and vain regrets. Hot words are bandied to and fro; the air resounds with angry shouts, and each one calls in turn on the wrathful gods for help. Then no player trusts another: "The pieces have been tampered with," they cry; and to have fresh ones they insist; and many a time, I've seen their faces bathed with tears. May Jove preserve from tantrums such as that, any woman who aims at pleasing us.

Such are the games which kindly Nature to your weakness doth vouchsafe. To man she opens forth an ampler field: to him the flying ball, the spear, the quoit and daring feats of horsemanship. You are not made to strive in contests on the field of Mars, or to plunge into the icy waters of the Virgin's spring, or into the tranquil current of the Tiber. But you may, and you would do well to do so, walk in the shade of Pompey's Portico when the fiery coursers of the Sun are entering the constellation of Virgo. Visit the temple sacred to Apollo, to the god whose brow is decked with the laurel, and who, at Actium, whelmed the Egyptian fleet beneath the wave; visit those stately buildings raised by the sister and wife of Augustus, and his son-in-law decorated with the naval crown. Draw near to the altars where incense is offered to the sacred cow of Memphis; visit our three theaters, splendid places for displaying your attractions; go to the arena still warm with blood new-shed, and that goal round which the chariots whirl with fiery wheel.

Things that are hidden no one heeds, and none desires what he has never known. What avails a beautiful face if none be there to see it? Even though you should sing songs more sweet than the songs of Thamyras and Amœbeus, who would praise the merits of your lyre, if there were none to hear it? If Apelles, of Cos, had not given us his vision of Venus, the goddess would still be buried beneath the waves. What does the poet long for? He longs for fame. That is the guerdon we look for to crown our toil. Time was when poets were the favorites of heroes and of kings, and in ancient days a choir of singers gained a rich reward. Hallowed was the dignity and venerable the name of Poet, and upon them great riches were often bestowed. Ennius, born in the mountains of Calabria, was deemed worthy of being buried nigh to thee, great Scipio. But now the poet's crown of ivy lies unhonored, and they, who through the hours of night do strictly meditate the Muse, are idlers held. Howbeit, they strive, and love to strive, for fame. Who would have heard of Homer if the *Iliad*—the deathless *Iliad*—had never seen the light? Who would have known Danaë if, for ever a prisoner, she had languished till old age came upon her in her tower?

You, my fair young charmers, will do well to mingle with the throng; bend your roaming footsteps full oft beyond your thresholds. The she-wolf has her eye on many a sheep before she selects her prey; the eagle pursues more birds than one. Thus a pretty girl should show herself in public. In the throng there is perhaps one lover in whom her charms will strike an answering chord. Wherever she be, let her show herself eager to please, and let her be mindful of everything that could enhance her charms. You never know when a chance may occur. Always have the bait ready. The fish will come and bite when you least expect it. It often happens that the dogs scour the woods and hills in vain, and then the stag comes of his own accord, and steps into the net. When Andromeda was chained to her rock, how was she to hope that any one should have compassion on her tears? Often a new husband is discovered at the old one's funeral: nothing makes a woman so alluring as to walk with disheveled hair and let her tears flow unrestrainedly.

But avoid the man that makes a parade of his clothes and his good looks, and is on the tenterhooks lest his hair should get ruffled. The sort of thing such men will tell you, they've said over and over again to other women. They're of the roving sort and never settle anywhere. What *can* a woman do when a man is more of a woman than she is, and perhaps has a bigger following of lovers? Perhaps you won't believe this, and yet it's perfectly true: Troy would still be standing, if the Trojans had listened to old Priam's advice. There are men who get on good terms with women by making out they love them; and having done so, proceed disgracefully to fleece them. Don't be taken in by their scented locks, their dandified clothes, their affected estheticism, and their much-beringed fingers. Perhaps the smartest of all these fine gentlemen is nothing but a crook, whose sole aim is to rob you of your fine clothes. "Give me back my property," is the burden of many a poor woman's complaint, whom some such ruffian has taken in. "Give me back my property," is what you are always hearing in every court of justice. And you, O Venus, and you, ye goddesses, whose temples grace the Appian Way, look down upon the scene unmoved. And some there are among these rakes, whose reputation is so blown upon, that any women who are taken in by them deserve no sympathy.

Women, learn, from the misfortunes of others, how to avoid a similar fate, and never let your door give admittance to a swindler. Beware, ye daughters of Cecrops, of paying heed to the protestations of Theseus! It wouldn't be the first time he had taken his solemn oath to a lie. And you, Demophoön, who inherited Theseus' gift for lying, how can we trust you, seeing how you broke your vows to Phyllis! If, my dears, your lovers bring you glittering promises, do the like to them; if they bring you presents, let them have the favors they have bargained for. A woman who, after receiving presents from her lover, withholds from him the pleasure that he has a right to, would be capable of extinguishing Vesta's eternal flame, of stealing the sacred vessels from the temple of Inachus, and of sending her husband to his last account with a glass of aconite and hemlock.

But come now, where am I getting to? Come, my Muse, draw in your reins a little, lest your steeds carry me beyond my goal. When your lover has paved the way with a brief note or two, and when your wide-awake maid has duly received and delivered them, read them over very carefully, weigh every word, and try to find out whether his love is merely pretense or whether he really means what he says. Don't be in too great a hurry to answer him; suspense, if it be not too prolonged, acts as a spur to love. Don't appear too accommodating to him, if he's a youngster; on the other hand, don't rap him too severely over the knuckles. Act in such a way as to instill him at once with hope and fear, and every time you say "No," make him think he'll have a better chance next time. What you write him should be ladylike, but simple and direct. Ordinary, unaffected language pleases the most. It often happens that a letter gives the necessary impulse to a hesitating heart; and how often too has some clumsy uncouth utterance completely neutralized a girl's good looks.

But you women who, though you don't aim at the honors of chastity, want to cuckold your husbands without their knowing it, be sure not to send your letters by any but a trusty hand. On no account send these evidences of your passion to an inexperienced lover. For failing to observe this precaution, I have seen young married women white with fear and spending their unhappy days in a condition of continuous slavery. Doubtless it is a shame for a man to keep such damning proofs; but they put into his hands weapons as terrible as the fires of Etna. In my idea, deceit should be countered by deceit, just as the law allows us to repel violence by violence. You should practice varying your handwriting as much as possible. Foul fall the knaves that compel me to give you such advice. And you should be sure and not write on a tablet that has been used, without making quite sure that the original writing has been quite rubbed out, lest the wax should give evidence of two different hands. The letters you write to your lover should be addressed as though to a woman, and you should always allude to him as *she, her*.

But let us leave these minor details for graver subjects; let us cram on all sail. If you want to retain your good looks, you must restrain your temper. Peace, gentle peace, is the attribute of man, as rage and fury are the characteristics of wild beasts. Rage puffs out the face, gorges the veins with blood, and kindles in the eye the fiery fury of the Gorgon. "Away with thee, miserable flute, thou deservest not that I should spoil my beauty for thee," said Pallas, when in the stream she beheld her distorted visage. And so with you. If any of you women looked at yourselves in the glass when you were in a raging temper, you wouldn't know yourselves, not one of you! Another thing, just as unbecoming, is pride. You must have a soft, appealing expression, if you want to attract a lover. Believe an old hand at the game. A haughty, disdainful look puts a man out of tune at once, and sometimes, even though a woman doesn't say a word, her countenance betrays something hostile and disagreeable. Look at whoever looks at you; smile back when you're smiled at; if any one makes signs to you, send back an answering signal. 'Tis thus that love, after making essay with harmless arrows, draws from his quiver his pointed darts. We also dislike gloomy women. Let Ajax love his Tecmessa. We are a jovial company, and we like a woman to be gay. As for you, Andromache, and you, Tecmessa, I should never have wanted either of you for a mistress; and beyond mere child-getting, I doubt whether your husbands sought, or found, any great pleasure within your arms. How can we imagine so dreary a woman as Tecmessa ever saying to Ajax, "O Light of my life," and all those other sweet things that charm us and console.

Let me be suffered to illustrate my own gay trifling art with examples from a much more serious affair. Let me compare it to the tactics of a general commanding an army. A leader that knows his business will entrust, to one officer the command of a hundred infantrymen, to another a squadron of cavalry, to another, the standards. Now you women should consider in what respect we can serve you best, and assign to each of us his special part. If a man's rich, make him give you presents; let the legal luminary give you his professional advice; let the eloquent barrister plead his lovely client's cause. As for us poets, we've got nothing to offer you but our verses; but what **we can** do better than the rest

of them is to love, and we spread far and wide the renown
of the charmer that has succeeded in captivating us. Nemesis
and Cynthia are famous names; Lycoris from East to West is
known, and now on every hand they want to know who is
this Corinna that I sing about. Perjury is hateful to a poet,
and poetry too is a great factor in the making of a gentle-
man. Ambition, love of riches, these things torment us not;
we reck not of the Forum and its triumphs; all we seek is
seclusion and repose. Love is swift to take hold of us and
burns us with its fiercest flame, and into our love, alas, we
put over-much of trust and confidence. The peaceful art
which we pursue lends a softness to our manners, and our
mode of life is consonant with our work. My fair ones,
never withhold your favors from the poets; the gods inspire
them and the Muses smile upon them. Aye, a god dwells
within us and we commerce with the skies. From the high
heavens doth our inspiration come. How shameful to expect
hard cash from a poet; yet it's a shame no pretty woman is
afraid to incur.

Learn how to dissemble, and don't display your avarice all
at once. Mind you don't lose a fresh lover when he realizes
the trap you are laying for him. A skillful groom doesn't
treat a colt just broken like a horse that has grown used to
harness. In the same way, you won't catch a novice with the
same snare as you use for a veteran. The one, a new recruit,
is fighting for the first time in his life beneath the standards
of love; he has never before been captured, and now that
you have snared him, you must let him know none but you.
He is like a young sapling, and you must surround him with
a lofty fence. Be sure to keep all possible rivals out of the
way. You will only retain your conquest if you share it with
no one. Love's dominion, like a king's, admits of no parti-
tion. So much for the novice. The other is an old cam-
paigner. His pace is slower and more deliberate. He will

endure many things that a raw recruit could never stand. He won't come battering in or burning down your front door. He won't scratch and tear his sweetheart's dainty cheek till the blood comes. He won't rend his garments, or hers either; he won't pull her hair out and make her cry. Such tantrums as that are only permitted in youngsters, in the heyday of youth and heat. But your older man is not a bit like that. He'll put up with all manner of snubs. He smolders with a small fire like a damp torch or like green wood fresh hewn on the mountain top. His love is more sure; the other's is more blithe, but it doesn't last so long. Be quick and pluck the fleeting blossom. Well, let us surrender the whole stronghold, lock, stock, and barrel. The gates have been flung open to the besiegers. Let them be easy in their minds. The traitor won't betray them. Now if too soon you yield, too soon you'll lose your love. Denials must be sometimes mingled with dalliance. You must sometimes keep your lover begging and praying and threatening before your door. Sweet things are bad for us. Bitters are the best tonic for the jaded appetite. More than one ship has sailed to perdition with a following wind. What makes men indifferent to their wives is that they can see them when they please. So shut your door and let your surly porter growl, "There's no admittance here!" This will renew the slumbering fires of love.

Now let us take the buttons off the foils, and to it with naked weapons; though, likely enough, I am instructing you for my own undoing. When you have netted your youthful novice, let him, at first, imagine he's the only one to enjoy your favors. But soon let him apprehend a rival. Let him think there's some one else with whom he has to share your charms. Some such tricks as these are needed, or his ardor would soon die down. A horse never runs so fast as when he has other horses to catch up and outpace. A slight gives a new life to our dying flame, and I confess that, for my own part, I couldn't go on loving unless I had a set-back to endure from time to time. But don't let him see so very much. Make him uneasy, and let him fear there's something more than just what meets his eye. Tell him that some imaginary servant always has his plaguey eye upon you. Tell him your husband's green with jealousy and always on the prowl. That will stimulate his ardor. A safe pleasure is a tame pleasure. Even if you were as free to have your fling as Thaïs, trump up some imaginary fears. When it would be easier for you to have him admitted by the door, insist on his climbing in at a window, and put on a scared expression when he looks at you. Then let some smart maid come rushing in crying, "We're ruined," and thrust him, trembling, into a cupboard. But sometimes let him have his pleasure of you undisturbed, lest he begin to ask himself whether the game is wholly worth the candle.

I was not going to touch on the methods of hoodwinking a cunning husband and a watchful guard. A wife should fear her husband; she should be well looked after; that is quite as it should be; law, equity, decency—all require it so. But that you should have to put up with such servitude, you who have just been freed by the Lictor's rod, that would be intolerable. Come to me, and I'll initiate you into the secret of giving them the slip. If you had as many warders as Argus had eyes, you shall, if you really are resolved, evade them all. For example, how is your warder going to hinder you from writing during the time you're supposed to be in your bath? Is he going to prevent a servant who is in your secrets and aids you in your amours from carrying your missives in her bosom under a wide shawl? Couldn't she stuff them in her stocking, or hide them under the sole of her foot? But suppose your warder checkmates all these subterfuges, let your confidante make her shoulders your tablets,

and let her body become a living letter. Characters written
in fresh milk are a well-known means of secret communica-
tion. Touch them with a little powdered charcoal and you
will read them. You may also do likewise with a stalk of
green flax, and your tablets will, unsuspected, take the invisible imprint of what you write. Acrísius did everything he
could think of to keep Danaë intact. Yet Danaë did what
she should not have done, and made a grandsire of him.
What can a woman's keeper do when there are so many theaters in Rome, when she can go sometimes to a chariot race,
sometimes to religious celebrations where men are not allowed
to show their faces? When the Bona Dea turns away from
her temples all men save, perchance, a few whom she has
bidden to come; when the unhappy keeper has to keep an eye
on his mistress's clothes outside the baths, in which, maybe,
men are securely hiding? And whenever she wants, some
friend and accomplice will say she's sick, and for all her ill-
ness accommodate her with the loan of her bed. Then, too,
the name of "adulterous" given to a duplicate key tells plainly
enough the use to which we ought to put it. Nor is the door
the only way to get into a woman's house. You can get the
keeper under, however prying he may be, by giving him a
good stiff drink; and even if you have to give him Spanish
wine, it's worth it. There are also potions that induce sleep
and cloud the brain with a darkness as heavy as Lethean
night. And your accomplice may usefully entice the pestilent fellow to hope for her favors, and by soft dalliance make
him oblivious of the fleeting hours.

But why should I teach you these tedious and minute devices when the man may be bought for a trifling tip. Presents, believe me, seduce both men and gods. Jove himself is
not above accepting a present. What will the wise man do,
when a very fool knows the value of a gift? A present will
even shut the husband's mouth. But only tip the keeper

once a year. When he's held out his hand once, he'll be
holding it out for ever. I lately complained, I remember,
that one must beware of one's friends. That unwelcome
statement was not addressed solely to men. If you are too
confiding, others will win the quarry that belonged to you
and some one else will net the hare that you had started.
That very kind friend, who lends you her room and her bed,
has more than once been on excessively friendly terms there
with your lover. And don't have too pretty servant-maids
about you either. More than one maid has played her mistress's part for me.

Oh, what a fool I am! Why do I let my tongue run away
with me like that? Why do I offer my naked bosom to be
pierced? Why do I betray myself? The bird doesn't tell the
fowler the way to snare her. The hind does not train the
hounds to hunt her. No matter; if only I can be of service,
I will loyally continue to impart my lessons, even if it means
another Lemnian outrage. Act then, my dears, in such a way
as to make us think you love us; there's nothing easier, for a
man readily believes what he wants to believe. Look on a
man seductively; keep sighing deeply; ask him why he's been
so long in coming; make out you're jealous; sham indignation; look as if you're weeping, and even scratch his face for
him. He'll very soon believe that you adore him, and as he
looks upon your sufferings he'll exclaim, "The woman's simply mad about me!" especially if he's a coxcomb and thinks
that even a goddess would fall in love with him. But if he
doesn't run quite straight himself, don't, whatever you do,
put yourself out too much about it. Don't go and lose your
head if you hear that you are not the only pebble on the
beach. And don't be in too much of a hurry to believe everything you hear. Think of Procris, and be warned by her
how dangerous it is to be too credulous.

Nigh the soft slopes of flowery Hymettus is a hallowed

fount whose lips are fledged with tender green; and all around low-growing shrubs form, not so much a wood, as a woodland brake; there the arbutus offers a kindly shelter; rosemary and laurel and the dark-leaved myrtle shed their perfume far and wide; there likewise grow the thick-leaved box, the fragile tamarisk, the humble clover and the soaring pine. The leaves of all these divers trees and plants, and the tips of the blades of grass, tremble in the breeze, set a-dance by the soft breath of the zephyrs. Hither young Cephalus, leaving his comrades and his dogs, would often come to rest his limbs o'erwearied with the chase; and here, he oft would say, "Come, gentle Zephyr, steal into my breast and cool the heat wherewith I am opprest." It happened once some busybody heard him and must needs report these harmless words unto his anxious spouse. Procris no sooner heard this name of Zephyr than, deeming Zephyr was some rival, she was stricken dumb with grief and fell into a swoon. Pale was she, pale as those belated clusters which, when the wine-harvest is over, whiten at the first touch of frost, or like those ripe quinces which bend down the branches with their weight, or like the wild cherry ere yet it is ripe enough for our tables. As soon as she came to herself, she rent the flimsy garments that covered her bosom and scored her face with her nails. Then swift as lightning, in a tempest of fury, her hair flying in the wind, she tore across the country like some fierce Mænad. When she reached the fatal spot, she left her companions in the valley, and treading stealthily, made her way boldly into the forest. What deed, O senseless Procris, dost thou meditate, hiding thyself thus? What fatal resolution arms thy distracted heart? Doubtless thou thinkest thou wilt see Zephyr, thine unknown rival, come upon the scene; thou thinkest with thine eyes to witness the unconscionable scene. Now dost thou repent thee of thy deed. For 'twere horror to surprise the guilty pair. Now dost thou glory in thy rashness. Love tortures thee and tosses thy bosom this way and that. All explains and excuses thy credulity: the place, the name, the story told thee, and that fatal gift that lovers have for believing that their fears are true. As soon as she saw the trampled grass and the print of recent footsteps, her heart beat faster than ever.

Already the noontide sun had curtailed the shadows and looked down at equal distances upon the East and West, when Cephalus, the son of the Cyllenian god, comes to the forest and bathes his face in the cool waters of a spring. Hidden close at hand, Procris, torn with suspense, gazes at him unseen. She sees him lie on the accustomed sward and hears him cry, "Come, thou sweet Zephyr, come thou cooling breeze." O what a joyful surprise is hers; she sees her error, and how a name had led her mind astray. Once more she is herself. Her wonted color comes again; she rises to her feet and longs to fling herself into her husband's arms. But as she rises, she makes a rustling in the leaves. Cephalus, thinking it some wild creature of the woods, quickly seizes his bow, and even now he holds in his hands the fatal shaft. What, O hapless one, art thou about to do? 'Tis no wild animal . . . stay thy hand! Alas, it is too late; thy wife lies low, pierced by the arrow thou thyself hast sped! "Alas, alas!" she cried. "Thou hast stricken the breast of one who loved thee. And now that Zephyr, who did cause me so to err, bears away my spirit in the breeze. Ah me, I die . . . at least let thy beloved hand close my eyelids." Cephalus, distraught with grief, bears in his arms his dying loved one, and with his tears doth bathe her cruel wound. Little by little the soul of rash Procris ebbs from her bosom, and Cephalus, his lips pressed close to hers, receives her dying breath.

But let us pursue our voyage and, so that our wearied bark may reach the haven at last, let us have done with illustrations and speak straight to the point. No doubt you are expecting me to conduct you to banquets, and you would like me to tell you what I have to teach you thereupon. Don't come too soon, and don't show all your graces till the torches are alight. Venus likes delay; and waiting lends an added value to your charms. Even if you were plain, eyes dimmed by wine would think you beautiful, and night would fling a veil over your imperfections. Take the food with the tips of your fingers; and you must know that eating is itself an art. Take care to wipe your hand, and don't leave dirty finger-marks about your mouth. Don't eat before meals when you are at home; and when you are at table, learn to be moderate and to eat a little less than you feel inclined to. If the son of Priam had seen Helen eating like a glutton, he would have taken to hating her. "What a fool I was," he would have said, "to have carried off such a thing as that!" It were better for a young woman to drink, rather than to eat, too freely. Love and wine go very well together. However, don't drink more than your head will stand. Don't lose the use of your head and feet; and never see two things when only one is there. It's a horrible thing to see a woman really drunk. When she's in that state, she deserves to be had by the first comer. When once she's at table, a woman should not drop off to sleep. A sleeping woman is a whore-son temptation to a man to transgress the bounds of modesty.

I am ashamed to proceed, but Venus whispers encouragingly in my ear. "What you blush to tell," says she, "is the most important part of the whole matter." Let every woman, then, learn to know herself, and to enter upon love's battle in the pose best suited to her charms. If a woman has a lovely face, let her lie upon her back; if she prides herself upon her hips let her display them to the best advantage. Melanion bore Atalanta's legs upon his shoulders; if your legs are as beautiful as hers, put them in the same position. If you are short, let your lover be the steed. Andromache, who was as tall as an Amazon, never comported herself like that with Hector. A woman, who is conspicuously tall, should kneel with her head turned slightly sideways. If your thighs are still lovely with the charm of youth, if your bosom is without a flaw, lie aslant upon your couch; and think it not a shame to let your hair float unbraided about your shoulders. If the labors of Lucina have left their mark upon you, then, like the swift Parthian, turn your back to the fray. Love has a thousand postures; the simplest and the least fatiguing is to lie on your right side.

Never did the shrine of Phœbus Apollo, never did Jupiter Ammon, deliver surer oracles than the sayings chanted by my Muse. If the art which I so long have practiced has aught of worth in it, then list to me; my words will not deceive you. So, then, my dear ones, feel the pleasure in the very marrow of your bones; share it fairly with your lover, say pleasant, naughty things the while. And if Nature has withheld from you the sensation of pleasure, then teach your lips to lie and say you feel it all. Unhappy is the woman who feels no answering thrill. But, if you have to pretend, don't betray yourself by over-acting. Let your movements and your eyes combine to deceive us, and, gasping, panting, complete the illusion. Alas that the temple of bliss should have its secrets and mysteries. A woman who, after enjoying the delights of love, asks for payment from her lover, cannot surely but be joking. Don't let the light in your bedroom be too bright; there are many things about a woman that are best seen in the dimness of twilight. Now, there, I've done; my pleasant task is o'er. Unyoke, for surely 'tis high time, the swans that have been harnessed this long while unto my car. And now, my fair young pupils, do as your youthful lovers did awhile ago; upon your trophies write, "Ovid was our master."

LOVE'S CURE

LOVE had read the title of this work. " 'Tis war," said he, "I see 'tis war that's now declared against me." O, Cupid, do not so accuse thy poet; do not so accuse me, who so oft beneath thy sway have carried the standards thou didst give into my care. No Diomede am I by whom thy mother was wounded when the steeds of Mars bore her, all bleeding, to her skyey home. Other youths oft burn with a languid flame; but I have always loved; and wouldst thou know what I am doing at this moment? Why, I am loving still! Nay, more than that: I have taught unto others the art of winning thy favors; I have shown how the promptings of blind passion should give place to the dictates of reason. Ah, no; none shall behold me going back upon my lessons, betraying thee, sweet child, recanting all that I have sung, and so destroying the work of my own hands.

Let every man who loves a woman that requites his love drink deep of his delight and spread his sails to prospering breezes. But if he is a hopeless wight that groans in the thraldom of an unworthy mistress, let him receive the assistance of my art so that he may escape from the toils. Wherefore would you have some poor unfortunate devil go and hang himself by a rope from a lofty beam and die a miserable death; or another plunge a dagger into his bowels? You, Cupid, are a lover of peace. The thought of murder fills you with horror. Now here is a man who, if he cannot cease to love, will die the miserable victim of an unhappy passion. Let him, therefore, cease to love, and you will not have his death upon your conscience. You are a child, and you should know of nought save merry sport. Be then king of the realm of play; 'tis a gentle scepter, suited to thy years. We know that thou hast many a keen arrow in thy quiver; but never are those arrows tinged with blood. Leave it to Mars, thy stepfather, to wage dire war with sword and spears; let him come forth victorious, stained with the foeman's gore; but as for thee, never engage in battles save those in which Venus, thy mother, has instructed thee to fight. They, at least, involve no risk to life and limb, and never have they caused a mother to bewail the death of a beloved son. So ordain it, if you will, that some one's door may be broken down in a nocturnal brawl, and that others may be adorned with many a wreath; grant that young men and timid maids may meet in secret embraces, and that, by hook or by crook, the suspicious husband may be deceived. Let the lover alternately beg and pray, and curse and swear, at his beloved's door. And when she repels him, let him sing his doleful plaint. Be satisfied with causing tears to flow; let tears be your toll, but never a life. Thy torch was never made to light the funeral pyre.

Thus spake I. And Love, stirring his gemmy wings, answered me and said, "Pursue thy self-allotted task." Come ye then and hear what I shall teach, unhappy youths whom your mistresses have deceived. To you I taught the art of love. Now learn from me the art of curing love. The hand that wounded you can also heal. The same soil brings forth the poisonous plants and likewise those that give balm and consolation. Often the rose beside the nettle blows. Telephus, the son of Hercules, had been wounded by the spear of Achilles, and that same spear did heal his wound.

And you, ye girls, list to what I tell you. Whatsoever things I teach are as useful to you as to your lovers. Arms we bestow on both opposing sides. If among the lessons that I inculcate, some there be of which you can make no use, they at least set forth examples whereby you may take profit. My aim is practical: it is to extinguish cruel flames, and from love's fetters to free the captive heart. Phyllis had never died so soon had I been her preceptor. Nine times she came to the Ocean's brink; she would have come and gone more often had I been there. Nor yet with dying eyes would Dido have seen, from her lofty citadel, the Trojans spreading their sails to the winds. Despair would never have made that mother turn her cruel hand against the fruit of her own womb; the mother who slew her own brood to avenge herself upon her perjured spouse. Thanks to my art, Tereus, though mad with love for Philomel, would never have deserved to be changed into a bird for his sins. Were Phasiphaë my pupil, she'd love her bull no more. And Phædra? She'd be cured of her incestuous passion. Suppose I had to deal with Paris? Menelaus would have no trouble with Helen; and Troy would never be conquered and fall into the hands of the Greeks. If only the impious Scylla had read my verses, Nisus had still retained his purple lock of hair. My brothers and sisters, hearken to my words. Give up all tragic, sinister passions. Take me for your pilot; your bark and its fraughting souls shall voyage in safety towards the haven. Ovid you doubtless read when you learnt the art of love. 'Tis Ovid again that you must read to-day. I am the public champion. I will remove that perilous stuff that weighs upon the heart. But let each and every one of you second the efforts I shall make on your behalf.

At the outset of my task, I invoke thee. Be thou to me propitious, O Apollo, who didst invent both Poetry and Medicine! Help thou in me the Poet, help the Physician, for I am both; and both these arts are under thy protection.

If you repent you of your love, stop on the threshold while you yet are able and ere yet your heart has been too deeply stirred. Suppress, ere yet they have gained too strong a hold, the evil signs of the sudden seizure; and at the very outset let your steed refuse to go another step. Time makes all things to increase; time ripens the grape upon the vine; it changes the blade of tender green into the sturdy stalk. The tree, that shelters the wayfarer beneath its spreading branches, was, when 'twas planted, but a feeble sapling. Then you might have dragged it from the surface of the soil; now it stands a mighty tree deep-rooted in the earth. Consider, in a rapid mental inventory, what it is you love, and withdraw your neck from the yoke that is bound one day to hurt you. Fight against it at the beginning. It is late in the day to make up physic when delay has given the disease time to get a hold on you. Make haste then, and don't put off till to-morrow the cure you can work to-day. If you are not ready to-day, to-morrow you will be less so. Love has always got its excuses and finds pretexts for delays. The first day that comes is not too soon to begin the cure. Rivers are never very broad near their source. It is the little tributaries that make them wide. If you had realized earlier how great a sin you were preparing to commit, never, Myrrha, would your features have been covered with the bark of a tree. I have known wounds which might easily have been cured if taken in hand at once, but which, through being neglected, grew past all healing. But we like to cull the flowers of pleasure, and every day we tell ourselves, "To-morrow will do just as well." Meanwhile the fire spreads along our veins, and the baneful tree drives its roots deep into the soil. If once the favorable moment has gone by, if Love has taken firm root in the heart, the physician's task is a far less easy one. But because I've been called in at a late hour, I must not for that reason leave the patient to his fate. When the hero, the son of Pœas, was wounded, he was compelled, with bold hand, to cut off the affected part; nevertheless he was cured, and report has it that it was he who, many years afterwards, ended the Trojan War.

A while ago I bade you take your malady in hand at once; now I bring you slow and tardy remedies. Endeavor, if you can, to master the fire at the outset, or, if you cannot, wait

till it has burnt itself out. When the fit of madness is at its
height, wait for the fit to pass. It is difficult to stop it in
mid career. Foolish is the swimmer who, though he can cross
a river by steering slantwise, insists on swimming right
athwart the current. An impetuous spirit, a man who, as
yet, is impatient of treatment, utterly refuses to listen to
advice. Wait till he will let you examine his wounds; wait
till he will listen to reason. Would any, save a madman, tell
a mother not to weep at the burial of her son? At such a
time as that, 'twere foolish to talk of resignation. When she
has given full rein to her grief, and eased the burden of her
affliction, then is the time, with words of consolation, to try
to soften the blow. The art of medicine, one may almost say,
is the art of choosing the moment to intervene. Given at the
proper time, wine is beneficial; otherwise it does harm. If
you don't undertake your treatment at the due and proper
stage, you do but inflame and aggravate the malady.

When, then, you feel in a due frame of mind to profit by
the assistance of my art, take my advice and eschew idleness.
Love is born of idleness and, once born, by idleness is fostered.
Sloth is at once the cause and nourishment of this sensuous
malady. Put sloth aside, and at once you break in twain the
shafts of Love; his torch is out, and henceforth is but a thing
for jest and mockery. As the plane tree loveth wine, as the
poplar loveth the pure stream, as the marshy reed loveth
slimy soil, so doth Venus delight in idleness. Love flees from
toil; if, then, you would banish love from your heart, find
some work for your idle hands to do and then you will be
safe. *Dolce far niente*, too much sleep, gambling, and over-
much wine-bibbing cloud the brain and, though they deal it
no serious wound, filch away its energy. Then Love, finding
the outposts all unmanned, captures the fortress at a blow.
Cupid and idleness are boon companions. He shuns indus-
trious folk. If your mind is unemployed, find work for it

to do. There are the Courts of Justice, there is the Law, there are your friends to be defended. Go forth and join the ranks of the candidates for civic offices; or join the forces and take part in warlike exercises. The pleasures of the senses will soon take to flight, a routed host. The fleeing Parthian offers you a chance to win distinction in the field. Score a double triumph over Love and over the Parthian and bring back your twofold trophy to the guardian deities of your country.

The instant Venus was wounded by the Ætolian's spear, she left it to her lover to carry on the war. Do you want to know why Ægisthus became an adulterer? The reason is plain: he had nothing to do. The other princes were detained at Troy in everlasting combats. Greece had transported all her forces into Asia. It was vain for Ægisthus to think of carrying on a war; there was none to carry on. Or of pleading at the Bar, there were no lawsuits in Argos. But he was unwilling to do nothing, so he did what he could; he made love. Thus it is that Love finds a way into our hearts, and takes up his abode there. The country, too, soothes our spirits, and the divers occupation of a farmer's life. There is no care that will not yield to these heart-healing tasks. Tame the steer and make him bow his neck beneath the yoke, in order that with the sharp ploughshare he may break the stubborn glebe. And when you've plowed your furrows, sow therein the grain of Ceres, which, in due time, the soil will give back to you with bounteous interest. See how the branches bend beneath their weight of fruit; how the trees may scarce sustain the load of good things they have produced! See how the streams flow on with a sweet murmur, and how the sheep browse on the tender grass! Yonder the goats seek the mountain crags and scarped rocks, soon to come home to their young with their udders heavy with milk. The shepherd modulates his song upon his rustic pipe; close

by him are his dogs, his trusty companions and the vigilant
guardians of his flock. Yonder the deep woods resound with
the lowing of kine. A heifer is crying for her lost calf. Shall
I tell of the bees driven forth by smoke placed underneath
their hives, so that their stores of honey may be removed?
With Autumn come the fruits; Summer is beautiful with the
ripening corn; Spring brings the flowers; and Winter, the
cheerful fireside. Year by year, as the season comes round,
the vine-dresser gathers the ripe grapes and treads out the
new wine beneath his feet. Year by year, in due time, we
see the harvester bind into sheaves the corn that he has
reaped, and clear the shorn field with his wide-toothed rake.
You can bed out plants in the moist loam of your kitchen-
garden, and make little channels of fresh water to flow
through it. And has the grafting season come? Then into
the branch insert the alien branch, and lo, the tree will deck
itself with borrowed leaves. When once these pleasures lay
their healing charm upon your soul, Love has no further
power to harm, and flutters away with weary pinion.

Then there are also the pleasures of the chase. Many a
time has Venus been put ignominiously to flight, vanquished
by Apollo's sister. Sometimes, accompanied by a hound with
a keen scent, you may hunt the flying hare; sometimes spread
your nets on the wooded slopes of the hills; scare the timid
stag by divers means, and lay the wild boar low, pierced with
thy huntsman's spear. Tired out, the night will bring thee
sleep and not desire of woman, and heavy slumber shall refresh thy limbs. There are other sports of a milder nature,
yet none the less diverting: you may go a bird-hunting—'tis
game of little value—and take them in nets, or snare them
with limèd twigs. You may also hide the bent hook beneath
the deceiving bait which the greedy fish devours apace. 'Tis
by such means as these, or others like them, that you may
beguile your time, until you have unlearned the art of love.

Above all, go far away; however strong the bonds that hold you back, leave the place. Go on a long journey. You will weep at the very thought of your mistress's name; you will stay your steps ere you have gone halfway. Never mind, the less you may wish to do so, the more resolutely you should hasten your flight. Keep on; force your reluctant feet to run. Fear, nor rain, nor sabbath, nor the tragic anniversary of the Allia; let nothing stop you. Never trouble your head about how far you've come; think how much farther you've got to go. Don't invent excuses for lingering about town. Don't count the days. Don't be always gazing towards Rome; but fly. The Parthian flies, and flying saves his skin from his adversary's blows.

My treatment, you say, is drastic. I know it is; but if you want to be cured, you mustn't mind putting up with a deal of pain in the process. When I've been ill, I've often forced myself, much against my will, to swallow the most horribly bitter physic, and they wouldn't let me have any of the things I craved for. Why, to cure your body you'd suffer any mortal thing; and won't you slake your thirst with a drop of cold water, won't you do anything to get your mind well again? Yet that is the most precious part of you. In the treatment I prescribe, it's only the beginning that is difficult; it's only the early stages that are so painful. See how the yoke galls the ox that bears it for the first time; even as the harness galls the newly-broken colt. Perchance it causes you a pang to quit your ancestral home. You will quit it, notwithstanding; yet ere long you will be fain to see it again. Nevertheless, 'tis not your home that calls you back, 'tis Love. Home-sickness is merely a pretext to conceal your weakness. Once you've started, the country, your traveling companions, the very distance you have come, will all tend to bring consolation to your spirit. But do not imagine it is enough to go away. You must stay away, in order that the fires which consume you may be extinguished and no spark lurk beneath the embers. If you are too impatient, if you return again before your mind has recovered its poise, Love will undo your efforts; all his dreadful might he'll turn against you anew. What if you have been away and return both hungry and thirsty? Your absence will but have added to your malady.

Let who will believe that magic and the noxious herbs of Hæmonia can be of any avail in love. Curses and spells have had their day. My Apollo, with his hallowed song, brings you lawful succor. No graves, at my command, will ope and wake their sleepers; nor will you see some ancient hag make the earth gape by the power of her unhallowed incantations; you will not behold the corn removed from one field to another, or the sun's orb suddenly grow pale. But the Tiber, as is his wont, will flow into the sea; and the Moon, drawn by her white steeds, will follow her customary path. Nay, 'tis not by magic spells that Love's malady shall be banished from thy heart; and Cupid will not be scared away by the fumes of burning sulphur.

What, O Maid of Colchos, did the herbs of the Phasian land avail thee when thou didst desire to remain in the home of thy fathers? And how, O Circe, did the herbs of Persa bestead thee when a favoring wind bore away the vessels of Ulysses? All didst thou do, so that thy crafty guest might not depart; nevertheless, unperturbed and unimpeded, he pursued his flight. Nought didst thou leave undone to allay the cruel fire that was devouring thee; still Love, for a long time to come, was to hold sway over thy reluctant breast. Thou, who couldst change men into countless divers shapes, hadst not the power to change the laws that ruled thy heart. 'Tis said that when Ulysses was making ready to depart, thou wast fain to restrain him with these words: "No more do I entreat thee to become my spouse, albeit I remember

I did, at first, conceive that hope. And yet, a goddess and the daughter of the Sun, it seemed to me that I was worthy to be thy wife. Oh, hasten not away, I do beseech thee; stay yet a little while, 'tis all I ask. What smaller boon than that could I implore? Look how high the seas are running; them oughtest thou to dread. Tarry awhile until the winds are favorable to thy sails. Wherefore wouldst thou flee? No new Troy is rising here. No one is calling his companions to arms. Here love and peace abide; here I alone suffer the pain of a grievous sorrow, and all this land shall be subject to thy sway." Thus spake she; but none the less Ulysses unmoored his bark; vain were her words, and, with his sails, the south wind wafted them away. But still the fires of her passion burned, and Circe betook her to her wonted arts. Howbeit they could not mitigate the violence of her love. Whoever then thou mayest be that seekest succor from our art, put not thy faith in witchcraft and incantations. But if some potent reason retains you in the capital, hearken to the advice which I shall give you for your sojourn there. Full of courage is he who can win his liberty at a blow and, bursting all the bonds that bind him, find, then and there, ease for all his pain. If there breathes a man so strong of soul, he will compel even my admiration, and I shall say: "That man is in no need of any help from me." But you who, sick at heart, would fain unlearn to love the woman whom you love; but cannot; and yet still would—you shall be my pupil. Often revolve within your breast the deeds of your erring mistress; and keep before your eyes the losses she has caused you. Say to yourself, "She has filched from me this thing and that and, not content with larceny, her extravagance has compelled me to sell my patrimony. What vows she made, and how often has she broken them! How often has she left me lying before her door! To others she gives her love, to me only her disdain. A common broker enjoys with her

the nights of love which she refuses me." Let all these griev-
ances embitter your feelings towards her. Recall them in-
cessantly to your mind, and let them sow the seeds of hatred
in it. And when you reproach her, may you wax eloquent;
but if only you grieve enough, eloquent you will be without
an effort. I was of late much occupied with a certain wench.
She was not, however, suited to my temperament. Like a
sick Podalirius, I was for curing myself with my own herbs,
and I confess that for a doctor I was a disgracefully bad
patient. I derived considerable benefit from continually
harping on the defects of my mistress. I persevered with
this treatment and it unquestionably did me good. "What
poor legs the girl has," I kept saying. Yet truth to tell, they
were nothing of the sort. "How very far from beautiful
are her arms." Yet truth to tell, they *were* beautiful. "How
squat she is." She wasn't. "What a lot of money she
wants." And that was, indeed, the main count in the in-
dictment. The good is often so near neighbor to the bad,
that we often confound the two and condemn as a fault
what is, in reality, a virtue. So far as you can, depreciate
the qualities of your mistress and warp your own judgment
by crossing, to her prejudice, the narrow limit betwixt good
and bad. If she's plump, say she's stodgy; if she's dark, say
she's a nigger; if she's slim, say she's a skeleton; if she's not
coy, say she's brazen; if she's modest, say she's a bumpkin.
Nay, further, endow her with accomplishments she conspicuously lacks, ask her, in the most persuasive manner in the
world, to display them. If she has no voice, urge her to
sing. If she can't move her arms with grace, beseech her to
dance. If her speech is uneducated, make her keep on talking to you. If she can't play a note, beg her to play. If
her breasts are covered with pimples, let there be no scarf
to conceal them. If her teeth are bad, tell her something
to make her laugh. Has she got watery eyes, tell her some-

thing to make her cry. It is also of service to appear before
her suddenly, in the morning, before she's had time to complete her toilet. A pretty dress delights us, gold and jewelry
cover a host of imperfections, and what one beholds of a
woman is the least part of her. Amid all her extraneous
adornments, it's no easy matter to find the genuine attractions. With the ægis of wealth does Love deceive the be-
holder. Take her unawares. You may do so with safety
to yourself. Her defects will suffice to dethrone her in your
eyes. But that is not always so, for it often happens that
"beauty unadorned's adorned the most" and captures many
lovers. Moreover, there is no offense against decency in
your putting in an appearance while she is smearing pomade
on her face. You'll find she's got boxes containing concoc-
tions of all the colors of the rainbow, and you'll see the paint
trickling down in warm streams on to her breasts. The
whole place stinks like Phineus' dinner-table, and I've often
felt as if I was going to be sick.

And now I'll tell you how to act when you're in the par-
oxysm of your pleasure. For Love, if you're going to win,
must be attacked on every side. There are some details,
however, which modesty will not permit one to describe;
but you will be clever enough to fill up the blanks. For
certain critics have recently come down rather heavily on
my books. They complain that my Muse is too unrestrained.
But so long as my work gives pleasure, so long as I am celebrated all the world over, it is of no importance to me what
one or two pettifoggers say about me. Even great Homer
was slandered by envious tongues. Whoever and wherever
you may be, Zoilus, Envy is your real name. Have not sacrilegious tongues outraged thy poems, thou whose genius
brought to our shores Troy and her conquered gods? Cal-
umny ever pursues the great, even as the winds hurl themselves on high places, and as Jove's thunderbolts strike the

mountain peaks. But you, whoever you may be, who are
offended by the licentiousness of my poems, try, if you can,
to acquire a sense of proportion. If we are going to sing
of mighty wars, then let us sing them in the manner of
Homer. But how could the pleasures of carnal love find
a place therein? Tragedy sounds the lofty note. Noble rage
should wear the tragic buskin. But our Muse should wear
a moderate heel. The iambus can go what pace it will, now
swift, now trailing its hinder foot, and is meet to be flung
at the opposing foe. But let mild Elegy sing of Cupids and
their quivers; she is a kindly mistress and should be suffered
to frolic as the fancy takes her. Achilles must not be sung
to the strains of Callimachus; and thy voice, O Homer, is
not the voice to sing of Cydippe. Who could bear to see
Thaïs enacting the rôle of Andromache? And whoever acted
Thaïs would cut a sorry figure as Andromache. But Thaïs
belongs appropriately to my art. If my Muse is one with
my subject, the victory is ours, and the charge brought
against me fails. Out on thee, devouring Envy! Great already is the fame I enjoy. It will be greater still if I continue as I have begun. But you haste away too fast. If I
do but live, you shall have many other causes of complaint,
for I have many and many a song yet to sing. For glory
delights me, and my zeal increases with my love of glory.
Our steed grows breathless at the beginning of the ascent.
Elegy tells me that she owes me as deep a debt as the Epic
owes to Virgil.

This is the answer to give to Envy. Now, draw in thy
reins, my poet, and revolve in thine own orbit. When you
are called to taste the delights of love and youthful dalliance, when the night of promised bliss approaches, then,
lest you should have too much joy of your mistress if you
go to her with a full quiver, find another charmer with
whom you may blunt the edge of your attack. The love

that follows love is not so fierce. But sweeter than any is
the love for which we have waited long. When it is cold,
we love the sun; when hot, the shade. Water is pleasant
to the parching tongue. I blush to say it, yet I *will* say it;
when you're about the act of love with your mistress, take
her in the posture that becomes her least. That will be easily
accomplished. Rare is the woman who tells herself the truth.
They deem themselves beautiful in every aspect. I bid you,
too, fling open wide the windows of her room, and in the
broad light of day, observe the blemishes of her body. But
when you have attained the goal of pleasure; when you are
o'erwearied both in body and in spirit; when your heart is
heavy; when you are wishing you had never touched a
woman, and deem it will be long ere you embrace another—
then note in the tablets of your brain all the defects that
you observe in her, and long let your gaze linger on her
imperfections. "Feeble resources these," some one perchance
will say. But means which, taken singly, are of no avail
are potent when conjoined. The bite of a tiny adder will
lay low a bull. Often a hound of modest size will hold a
boar at bay. Gather all these remedies together; numbers
will win.

But seeing that temperaments, like faces, are infinitely
varied, use your judgment and follow not my behests too
blindly. A thing which, in your eyes, might convey no
offense, in another's might be quite unpardonable. Some
men have known their ardor checked because they've seen
unveiled those parts which modesty should hide; others because, leaving the bed wherein they've had their joy, they
have perceived the unclean traces of the fray. Ye who could
be deterred by trifles such as these, your love was but a jest:
feeble the flames that warmed your breasts. Well, let the
wingèd boy bend his bow more fiercely; then, more sorely
stricken you'll come in multitudes to beg for stronger medi-

cine. What shall I say of him who hides that he may behold his mistress performing her natural needs, and see those things which decency forbids that we should look upon? God forbid that I should counsel anything so vile as that. Even were they effectual, such means should never be essayed.

I would counsel you also to have two mistresses at a time. If you could have more, it would be still better. When your heart is thus divided between two loves, the two passions mutually moderate each other. The mightiest rivers lose their force when split up into several streams; the fire dies down when you take away the fuel that feeds it. One anchor will not hold several ships, and you should always fish with more than one hook in the water. The man who has taken the precaution to have two strings to his bow has thereby made his final victory sure. But if you have been so rash as to confine your affections to a single mistress, lose no time now in adding to the number. Minos extinguished his flame for Pasiphaë by conceiving a passion for Procris. His second consort banished his memory of the first. The brother of Amphilochus, lest he should love for ever the daughter of Phegeus, made Callirhoë the partner of his couch. Œnone would have held Paris captive for ever had she not been supplanted by the adulterous queen of Sparta. The Odrysian tyrant would have continued faithful to his spouse, had not Philomela outrivaled her sister in beauty. But wherefore should I linger over examples, examples so many that it would weary me to cite them? A new love always triumphs over the one it follows. A mother with several children bears more easily the death of one of them than she who cries, in bitter sorrow, "My son, my son, I had but thee!"

Think not that herein I am expressing any new ideas. The son of Atreus, long before me, was familiar with this truth; and what did he not allow himself, that prince who

was lord paramount of the whole of Greece! He loved his
captive Chryseis whom as a victor he had taken as his spoil.
But the maiden's father filled all the region round with his
sorrowful lamentations. Wherefore weepest thou, wretched
old man? They are getting on famously together, and you
do but hurt your daughter with your ill-timed importunities.
At last, relying on Achilles to support him, Calchas demands
that she should be set at liberty, and she returns to her
father's roof. Then said Agamemnon, "There is another
maiden no less fair than her, whose name, save for the first
syllable, is identical with hers. Let Achilles, if he be wise,
yield her up to me; or if he does not, he shall feel the power
of my dominion. If any one among you, men of Greece,
shall dare to blame my conduct in this matter, he shall learn
what the scepter wielded by a strong hand can accomplish.
For if, king as I am, I do not win her to share my bed, then
let Thersites take my place upon the throne." Thus he spake.
In place of Chryseis, who had been snatched from him, he
took this slave, and in the arms of Briseis he forgot his former love.

Follow then the example of Agamemnon. Seek like him
another object for your passion, and between two rival mistresses let your love, uncertain, hover. You ask me where
you are to find them? Go read my Art of Love, voyage
on, confident and fearless, and soon your bark shall be laden
with pretty women. If my precepts are of any avail, if, by
my voice, Apollo teaches aught that may be of use to mortal
men, when your despairing heart is consumed with a passion
fiercer than the fires of Ætna, act in such a manner that your
mistress may deem you colder than ice. Pretend that you
are cured, and if your heart still bleeds, never let her suspect
it. Let laughter be upon your lips, though tears be in your
heart. I do not bid you break with her in the very height
of your passion. I lay upon you no mandate so severe as

that. But learn to dissemble. Assume a calmness, if you
have it not, and soon you'll really be as calm as now you
feign to be. Often, so that I might drink no more, I've
feigned to be asleep, and, in the midst of feigning, I've
fallen asleep indeed. It's made me laugh sometimes to see
how a man, acting the passionate lover, has, like an unskilled
hunter, fallen into his own net.

Love steals into our hearts, as it were, by habit; by habit
also we can school ourselves to forget it. If you can pretend you're cured, cured you will be indeed. Your mistress,
say, has promised you to lie with her a certain night. Go
to her house. When you get there, you find the door barred
and bolted against you. No matter. Be patient. Neither
beg nor pray; but lie not down beside the cruel door. Next
morning, never utter a reproach; and on your countenance
wear no sign of grief. Seeing your cool indifference, she'll
lay aside her arrogant disdain. That is some good, and for
it you will have my art to thank. But try, and stint not,
to deceive yourself, until you have forgot the way to love.
A steed will oft refuse the bit that's offered him. Hide, even
from yourself, the reason of your tactics, and, all uncon-
sciously, you'll reach your goal. The bird is scared by the
net when it is too plainly visible. So that your mistress may
not push her pride to the point of disdain, be round with
her, and her arrogance will melt before your own. If you
find her door open, as though by chance, and if she summons
you by name again and again, pass by and take no heed. If
she offers you an assignation for a given night, look doubtful
and say, "I'm very much afraid I shall be unable to come."
A man should easily be able to lay this discipline upon himself, if he's endowed with reason. Besides, you can always
go and find immediate consolation in the arms of some
woman of the town.

It could hardly be said that my treatment was too severe,

seeing that I make it my object to reconcile pleasure and good sense. But as people and dispositions are infinitely varied, so must our treatment be varied too. A thousand ills require a thousand cures. There are some illnesses which demand an operation; others which the juice of a herb will heal. If you are too weak to go away, do not attempt to shake off your fetters. Has cruel love got his foot upon your throat? Give up the hopeless fight. Let the wind waft your vessel, and with your oar assist the waves that bear you along. You say you must find something to allay the thirst that consumes you? Well and good; you must. Drink then your fill, from the very middle of the river. Drink, not enough but too much, so that you vomit what you have taken in. Enjoy your mistress, drink unhindered of her charms. Spend your nights, your days, with her. Drink of her till you're sick. Satiety will cure you of your ills. Stay with her even when you think you could leave her without a pang. Never quit the house, which you have begun to hate, until you are worn out with those pleasures which excess has now turned to gall and wormwood in your heart. Love that is fed by jealousy dies hard. He who would banish love, must banish, first, mistrust. A man who is for ever on thorns lest he should lose his mistress, or fears that some rival will filch her from him, even Machaon himself could scarcely cure. If a woman has two sons and one of them is at the wars, 'tis he that is in danger whom she loves the more.

There is, hard by the Collinian gate, a venerable temple to which the lofty Eryx gave its name. There reigns a deity whose name is Oblivion. He gives unfailing succor to the sick; he dips his torch into the cold waters of Lethe. Thither come young men and maidens, the victims of unrequited love. Thither they come to seek oblivion for their sorrow. This god (was it indeed a god, or but the shadow of a dream?), this god spake to me and said, "O Ovid, thou who alternately dost kindle and extinguish the restless flames of love, add this precept to thy lessons. Let but a lover ponder on all the ills that threaten him, and he will love no more. To all of us hath the god allotted more or less of ills. Whoso fears the Puteal and Janus and the swift-coming Kalends, the sum of money he has borrowed shall be his torment. The man that has a stern unbending father, even if all else be in accordance with his wishes, will ever have that father before his eyes. The man who has married a dowerless wife, and passes his days in poverty, will think his wife an obstacle to his success. Have you a vineyard where the grapes grow ripe on a rich soil? Beware lest the swelling grape be blighted. Another man has a ship on its way home: he will be always reminding himself that the sea is treacherous and fearing that the shore is strewn with his lost merchandise. Another man fears for his son on active service; another for his daughter, who is ripe for marriage. Who has not innumerable reasons for anxiety? Perchance you would have hated your mistress, Paris, if the death of your brothers, and the way they died, could have been brought before your eyes." The god was still speaking when his childlike image vanished with my dream: if indeed he, too, were not a dream.

What am I to do? Abandoned, without a helmsman, amid the welter of waters, my bark drifts at random over uncharted seas. Lover, whosoever thou art, shun solitude: solitude for you is dangerous. Wherefore shouldst thou avoid it? Because you will be safer amid the throng. 'Tis not well for you to be alone. Solitude increases the torments of love. You will find it will ease the burden of your heart to mix freely with your fellows. If you remain alone, melancholy will descend upon you. The vision of your forsaken mistress will be ever present to your eyes; you will imagine that you see her before you in the flesh. That is why the

night is sadder than the light of day. There is no company
about you then, no troops of friends, to help you banish
your sorrows. Do not shut yourself up indoors; do not go
and hide your tear-stained visage where none may see it. Let
Pylades be ever at hand to comfort his Orestes. In such
circumstances, a trusty friend is a great resource. What
was it but the loneliness of the woods that brought such
woe to Phyllis? There is no doubt that solitude was the cause
of her death. She rushed with disordered tresses, like one
of those Bacchantes who every three years celebrate the feast
of Bacchus on the Aonian hills. Sometimes she gazed out
over the waste of waters; sometimes she flung herself down
upon the sandy shore, fordone with weariness. "Faithless
Demophoön," she cried to the unheeding waves; and her lamentations were broken by her sobs. By a narrow path, over-
hung with thick foliage, she often made her way to the seashore. And now she had just come thither for the ninth
time. "The die is cast!" she cried. The color left her cheeks,
and she looked down at her girdle. She gazed also at the
trees round about. Her courage faltered. She shuddered,
and many times she clutched her throat with her hands.
Ah, hapless Phyllis! Would to heaven thou hadst not been
alone in that hour! The woods, that mourned thy death,
would not have shed their leaves in grief for thee. And
you, to whom your mistress has been unkind, or you, my
fair one, jilted by your lover, think of Phyllis; be wise in
time, and beware of too much solitude.

A certain young man of my acquaintance had religiously
followed the advice of my Muse; he was just reaching port;
he was virtually safe when the unexpected encounter of two
passionate lovers carried him out to sea again. Love had
only been hiding his shafts; and he quickly seized them again.
Whoever you may be, if you would recover from your
malady, keep clear of other people who are suffering from

it. It is horribly contagious: you've only got to look at some other sufferer's wounds, and you feel as if you had been hit yourself. Many ailments are spread in this way. It often happens that a dry and barren field suddenly becomes fertile, being watered by a stream that has changed its course. Similarly Love glides imperceptibly into our hearts; that is, if we don't keep clear of lovers. But, in this regard, every man-jack of us is an adept at self-deception. I know a man who had recovered; it was the next-door neighbor that brought on his relapse. Another man ran across his mistress by accident. It was too much for him. The wound hadn't properly healed: it opened again, and all my skill was useless. It's no easy matter to protect yourself against fire when the house next door is burning. It's just as well to keep out of harm's way. Don't go near the portico where she is wont to walk; and don't let any duty visits cause you to run the risk of seeing her. What's the good of trying to blow the smoldering embers into flame. You would do better to go and live in another hemisphere if you could. If you're fasting, it's not easy to keep away from a table that's laid for dinner; and the sound of running water is a mighty stimulant to thirst. It takes a lot to hold in a bull when he catches sight of a heifer, and your doughty stallion always neighs when he sees a mare.

When, after a deal of buffeting, you're just getting into harbor, it is not enough to give up your mistress, you must likewise keep out of the way of her mother, her nurse, her bosom friend; in short, of any one and every one connected with her. Mind some slave or servant-girl doesn't come with some message to you, and sham weeping as she delivers it. And don't, out of curiosity, inquire how she's getting on. It's dangerous. Hold your tongue: it will pay you. And don't go counting up the reasons you have had to break with your mistress. Give up accusing her. Silence will be the best

way to pay her out; so keep silence till you don't care any
more about her. It's far better to say nothing than to go
about telling people you are no longer in love. The man
who says to everybody, "I don't love her any more," is still
in love. The best way to get a fire under is to tackle it
methodically, steadily and surely. It's no good trying to
smother it all at once. Drop her gradually. You'll reach
safety in the end. A mountain stream is more impetuous
than a river, but the course of the torrent is soon run; the
river flows far and ceaselessly. Your love should be like a
cloud, it should gradually melt away into the air. It's a bru-
tal thing to hate a woman one day whom you worshiped the
day before. To make such a sudden change as that, you'd
have to have the heart of a barbarian. Just give up paying
her attentions; that's enough. If a man finishes up by hating
a woman, he's either really still in love with her, or else he's
in a frame of mind for which he won't easily find a cure.
It is a disgraceful thing that a man and a woman, who were
but lately head over ears in love, should suddenly become at
daggers drawn. Even Themis disapproves of conduct such
as that. A man will often bring an action against a woman
and, notwithstanding, still be in love with her. When love
leaves no resentment in its train, it departs quite quietly
and peaceably. The other day I had fallen in with a young
acquaintance of mine. His mistress was close at hand in a
litter. He was upbraiding her with the most violent reproaches. Just as he was about to serve his writ he exclaimed,
"Let her descend from her litter." She did so, and no sooner
had he set eyes upon her than he was another man. His
hands dropped to his side; his tablets fell from his hands.
He flung himself into her arms, crying, "You have won!
You have won!" It's much wiser and much surer to let
things drop peaceably than to quit the bed for the law-
courts. Let her keep the presents you have given her, with-

out making a fuss. It's very often well worth while to make
a slight sacrifice. And then, if by chance you do happen to
run across her, be sure and make use of the weapons with
which I have armed you. So, be of good cheer! Fight the
good fight! Penthesilea will get the worst of it. Remember
your fortunate rival; think of the door banged and bolted
in your face; and think of all the lies your mistress has told
you, and all her broken vows. Don't take a lot of extra
trouble over your hair because you have to meet her, or
spend ages getting yourself up regardless of expense. Don't
worry about the impression you're going to make on a woman
who henceforth is going to be a stranger to you. Just treat
her as you would treat an ordinary acquaintance.

Shall I tell you what is the greatest obstacle to our success? Well, it's this. We give up our mistresses too late,
because we flatter ourselves that we are still the object of
their affections. Our self-conceit adds fuel to our credulity.
Don't believe in vows, there's nothing more misleading; and
don't trust their sacred oaths. Beware of being moved by
their tears. They've learnt the art of weeping. A lover's
heart is a prey to countless artifices; it is like the pebble on
the beach, tossed hither and thither by the waves of the
sea. Don't proclaim the reasons which impel you to break
it off. Don't prate about your grief, and go on grieving
in secret. Don't reproach her with her misdeeds, for fear
she should justify them. On the contrary, play a generous
game with her, so that her case may seem better than your
own. The strong man is the silent man. If you heap insults upon her, you're inviting her to justify herself.

I am not going to rival the King of Ithaca. I should
never dare, like him, to plunge Love's arrows and flaming
torches into the river. I shall not clip his roseate wings, nor
would I aim at slackening his sacred bow. The object of
my song is but to give advice. Follow the counsels I give,

and do thou, O Phœbus, the Healer, continue, as you have done hitherto, to smile upon my efforts. Lo! Phœbus is here: I heard his lyre, I heard his quiver sound. By those signs I recognize the god. Lo! Phœbus is at hand, and he will lend his aid!

Compare a stuff dyed with Tyrian purple to something dyed at Amyclæa. You wouldn't look at the latter. In the same way, let every one of you compare his mistress with the illustrious beauties of the world, and he will blush for her. Paris thought Juno and Minerva were beautiful till he had seen Venus; after that, they were nowhere. And don't think merely of the face. Take character and accomplishments into account. And don't let love blind your judgment.

The remedy that I am now going to propose to you is a little thing; yet despite its trifling nature, it has stood more than one lover in good stead, myself first of all. Do not keep, and read over, the letters your mistress has written you. The strongest resolution would be shaken by such a test. Never mind how great the pang it may cause you, give them to the flames, and, as you do so, say, "Thus may this fire destroy my love also." The daughter of Thestius, with the aid of an ember, burnt up her absent son. Will you then think twice before you cast these lying missives into the fire? Banish too, if you have strength of mind enough, the counterfeit presentment of her. Why keep doting on a lifeless image? 'Tis that that was Laodamia's undoing. Then there are certain places you must shun. Avoid the scenes where you have had her in your arms; they will be full of bitter memories for you. "It was there she used to sit. She used to lie there. There is the bed in which I slept with her arms about me; here, one night of pleasure, she gave me rapturous delight." Such recollections reawaken love. The old wound, not yet properly healed, opens again.

Convalescents should never run risks. If you bring sulphur near an ember that is not quite extinguished, the fire springs up anew; a spark becomes a conflagration. So too, if you do not take care to avoid everything that might resuscitate your passion, you'll find the embers you think dead, flaming up once more. The Grecian fleet would fain have fled from Capherea and the misleading beacon which thou, old Nauplius, didst kindle to avenge the death of thy son. Glad at heart is the cautious mariner when he has passed through the straits of Scylla. Beware then of those regions which once were sweet to you. They may be your Syrtes. Avoid the rocks of Acroceraunia: 'tis here that cruel Charybdis ceaselessly spews forth again the waters that she swallows.

There are other remedies which one can hardly advise you to employ of your own free will, but which, when they chance to come one's way, are often potent in their effect. Let Phædra but lose her riches and Neptune will spare his grandson, nor will he suffer the monstrous bull to terrify the horses of Hippolytus. Had Pasiphaë been reduced to poverty, she would have loved less inordinately. Voluptuous love is fostered by riches. Why did no man take Hecale, and no woman Irus? Because he and she were poor. Poverty has not the wherewithal to nourish love. Howbeit, this is no sufficient reason why you should wish to be poor. But this, at all events, is important, and you should bear it in mind: Never go to the theater until Love has been completely ousted from your heart. The sound of flutes and lyres and the human voice, and arms waved in time to the music, are sore enervators of the mind. Fictitious loves are continually being represented there.

It behoves me that I should, by my art, teach you what to avoid and what to cultivate. It pains me to say so; but have nought to do with poets who sing of love. I am robbing my own children of their birthright. Flee from Callimachus, for

no enemy of love is he; and thou too, poet of Cos, thou work-
est ill, even as Callimachus. Sappho, of a surety, made me
sweeter towards my mistress; nor did the poet of Teos impart
rigidity to my morals. Who could read the poems of Tibullus without danger, or the verses of that bard who made
Cynthia the sole burden of his song? Who could leave the
reading of Gallus with heart untouched? And in my verses,
too, there is an influence, I know not what, that prompts to
love. But if Apollo, the god who is my guide, deceives not
his singer, the greatest cause of our ills is a rival. Beware,
therefore, of conjuring up to yourself the image of a rival,
and resolutely persuade yourself that your mistress sleeps
alone. What added fire to the passion of Orestes for Hermione was that she had taken another for her lover. Wherefore, Menelaus, dost thou grieve? Thou didst go without thy
spouse to Crete, and wast able to remain a long while apart
from her. But since Paris carried her off, you have not been
able to live without your Helen. Your love for her was in-
creased by another's. What made Achilles weep the more
bitterly when Briseis was taken from him was that she was
transferring her charms to the couch of Plisthenes. And, believe me, he had reason for his tears. The son of Atreus did
what any man was bound to do if he were not grossly in-
active. He did what I should have done, had I been he, and
I am no wiser than he. That was the choicest fruit of this
case of jealousy. For when Agamemnon swore by his scepter
that he had never touched Briseis, he never bethought him
that his scepter was divine.

The gods grant that you may be able resolutely to pass
your late mistress's door, and that your feet may not belie
your determination. And you *will* be able, if your will
power is strong enough. But you must go on firmly, and dig
the spurs deep into your horse's sides. Make believe that her
house is a den of Lotophagi, a cave of Sirens. Crowd on full

sail and row with all your might.   It would be well, too, if
you could bring yourself to look with calm indifference on
the rival who lately caused you such an agony of grief.   Even
if you retain a particle of hate towards him, at least give him
a civil nod.   When you are able to embrace him, your cure
will be complete.

Now, as a sound doctor should, I am going to give you a
few hints about diet, about the things to eat and the things
to avoid.   Everything of a bulbous nature, whether from
Daunia, Libya, or Megara, you should shun like poison; and,
just as religiously, you should avoid rocket and all such
aphrodisiacs.   You would find it beneficial to take rue, which
clears the sight, and anything, in general, of a sedative nature.
What about wine, you ask?   I'll put the whole thing in a
nutshell for you.   Wine promotes sexual desire, provided you
don't drink to intoxication.   Wind fans a fire into flame;
wind also puts it out.   Either don't drink at all, or drink
enough to drown your troubles.   Half-way measures are
injurious.

And now my task is o'er.   Crown my wearied bark with
garlands.   I have reached the haven towards which I set my
course.   Young men and pretty girls, healed by my song,
you will soon be rendering pious thanks to your poet.

THE ART OF BEAUTY

NOW learn, my dears, the art of beautifying your faces; learn by what means you can retain your charms. Cultivation makes the sterile ground bring forth fruit; it destroys the thorny brambles. Cultivation softens the sourness of the apple, and the grafted tree bears fruit both rich and strange. Art clothes all things with beauty. Lofty ceilings are gilded with gold; the dark soil is hidden by the marble edifices raised upon it. The fleeces are dyed many times in the brazen cauldrons with Tyrian purple, and ivory from India is carved and cut to suit the luxury of our times.

Maybe, in those far-off days, when Tatius was king, the Sabine women thought more of dressing the fields of their forefathers than of dressing themselves. In those times, the red-faced matron, perched clumsily on her high stool, would spin and spin the livelong day. She put into the shed the flocks her daughter brought home from the meadows; she tended the fire herself by heaping furze and faggots on it. But your mothers' daughters are daintier and more refined than that. You must needs have dresses embroidered with gold; you like to do your perfumed hair in countless different ways; you must have sparkling rings upon your fingers. You adorn your necks with pearls brought from the East, pearls so big that your ears can scarcely bear the weight of them. Nevertheless we must not reproach you with the care which you bestow upon your person, since the men, in these days, pay immense attention to their dress. The men take a leaf out of the women's book, and the wives can hardly outdo their husbands in luxurious attire.

Thus then let every woman strive to look her best. It matters not how love shall spread its lure. Tasteful simplicity no one can find fault with. There are women who, though buried in the country, are yet most careful about their hair. Even if rugged Athos should hide them from view, they would dress well—for Athos. They even take a pleasure in dressing to please themselves, and every young girl loves to make the most of her attractions. The bird of Juno, when his plumage is praised, spreads out his tail to be admired, and dumb though he be, is proud of his beauty. To kindle in us the fires of love, dress is more potent than the dread arts of the magician. Trust not to herbs, nor to philters compounded of divers juices, and essay not the flux of the mare on heat. Serpents are not cut in two by the incantations of the Marsians; and rivers no longer flow backwards to their sources. You may bang the brass of Temesa as much as you will, it will never bring down the moon to earth.

Your first preoccupation, my dears, should be your manners. When a woman's manners are good, she never fails to attract. Manners indeed are more than half the battle. Time will lay waste your beauty, and your pretty face will be lined with wrinkles. The day will come when you will be sorry you looked at yourself in the mirror, and regret for your vanished beauty will bring you still more wrinkles. But a good disposition is a virtue in itself, and it is lasting; the burden of the years cannot depress it, and love that is founded on it endures to the end.

Now, when you have had your full of sleep, and your delicate limbs are refreshed, come learn from me how to impart a dazzling whiteness to your skin. Strip of its straw and husk the barley which our vessels bring to our shores from the fields of Libya. Take two pounds of peeled barley and an equal quantity of vetches moistened with ten eggs. Dry the mixture in the air, and let the whole be ground beneath the mill-stone worked by the patient ass. Pound the first horns that drop from the head of a lusty stag. Of this take one-sixth of a pound. Crush and pound the whole to a fine powder, and pass through a deep sieve. Add twelve narcissus bulbs which have been skinned, and pound the whole together vigorously in a marble mortar. There should also be added two ounces of gum and Tuscan spelt, and nine times as much honey. Any woman who smears her face with this cosmetic will make it brighter than her mirror.

Then make haste and bake pale lupins and windy beans. Of these take six pounds each and grind the whole in the mill. Add thereto white lead and the scum of ruddy niter and Illyrian iris, which must be kneaded by young and sturdy arms. And when they are duly bruised, an ounce should be the proper weight. If you add the glutinous matter wherewith the Halcyon cements its nest, you will have a certain cure for spots and pimples. As for the dose, one ounce applied in two equal portions is what I prescribe. To bind the mixture and to make it easy of application, add some honey from the honeycombs of Attica.

Although incense is pleasing to the gods and soothes their wrath, it must not be kept exclusively for their altars. A mixture of incense and niter is good for black-heads. Take four ounces of each. Add an ounce of gum from the bark of a tree, and a little cube of oily myrrh. Crush the whole together and pass through a sieve. Bind the resultant powder by mixing with honey. Some people recommend that fennel should be added to the myrrh; nine scruples of myrrh and five of fennel is the proportion. Add a handful of dried rose-leaves, some sal-ammoniac and male frankincense. Pour on barley-water, and let the weight of the sal-ammoniac and the incense equal the weight of the roses. After employing very few applications of this mixture, you will have a charming complexion.

I have seen a woman pound up poppies soaked in cold water and rub her cheeks with them. . . .

The UNIVERSAL *Library*

OCCUPATION: WRITER

By

ROBERT GRAVES

OCCUPATION: WRITER *is not a how-to-write manual. It is more like a roller-coaster ride through one of the most astonishing minds of our times. But the title is accurate as far as it goes: Robert Graves has established himself at the top of his profession with a solid body of achievement in all literary forms over more than three decades. The general public knows him for his best-selling novels, which, though they deal with history, bear about the same relation to the genre of the "historical novel" as the "Iliad" might to the* BOBBSEY TWINS. *Scholars know him as one of the most penetrating searchers and fecund interpreters of man's past. Graves regards himself as a poet. Lesser poets may well regard him as a magician, for he seems to have an almost eerie familiarity with the Muse herself.*

In this collection of shorter pieces are lusty humor, as in THE LOST ART OF SWEARING, *erudition combined with wit, as in* IMPERIAL INCEST, *light satire, as in* THE ANCESTORS OF COLONEL BLIMP, *and "a selected number of theatrical pieces, short stories, and other elegant trifles calculated to delight the most discriminating of ladies and gentlemen."*

UL-53

THE TASTEMAKERS
By
RUSSELL LYNES

"TASTE," *says the author of this book, "is our personal pleasure, our private dilemma and our public facade."* THE TASTEMAKERS *is the lively story of the people and pressures that have shaped American taste for the last dozen decades.*

In a serious but witty and perceptive account, Mr. Lynes gives the battles of the taste-makers the dignity or humor they deserve — battles that are sometimes solemn and full of conviction, sometimes pompous, sometimes gay and frivolous. He reanimates — with all their original intensity and excitement — the battles of taste that account for our likes and dislikes today.

"It is a highly original job, very sound in schol-arship, very sagacious, and constantly amusing. ...The way he lightly transforms himself into an encyclopedia of American culture is delightful and a little breathtaking." BERNARD DEVOTO

"It reads like the liveliest conversation of a wise friend—the sort of conversation one always wishes would find its way into a book." HERBERT AGAR

UL-54

WITH NAPOLEON IN RUSSIA
By
ARMAND DE CAULAINCOURT

IN AUGUST, 1933, an architect looking among the ruins of General Armand de Caulaincourt's old chateau in Picardy, noticed a battered iron chest in a pile of debris. On opening the chest he discovered the long-lost original manuscript of General de Caulaincourt's fabulous memoirs. Upon study, these memoirs turned out to be the most important discovery of Napoleonic materials in our time, for in them was a complete eye-witness account of how the Emperor planned and fought his greatest and most disastrous war—his invasion of Russia.

No book on Napoleon has more bearing on the events of today than this astounding chronicle of the struggle between the Emperor and the Czar. Here is revealed not only the thoughts and actions of the great Emperor as recorded by his most distinguished aide and confidant, but also startling insights into the enigmatic character and ways of the Russians, whom Caulaincourt knew well since he had been Ambassador to the court of St. Petersburg.

Scholars and students will find fascinating parallels in the events of then and now. They will also find within these pages the most vivid closeup of Napoleon that we possess, the picture of a man considered a deity by many, possessed of the most remarkable qualities of leadership, yet prisoner of irrational obsessions that led him to defeat.   UL-55

THE COMEDIES OF
OSCAR WILDE

THE COMEDIES *of Oscar Wilde have delighted audiences for more than half a century. As examples of wit and cynicism fashioned with the most glittering insolence, they are unsurpassed, and belong in the tradition of English high-comedy which has come down from Congreve through Goldsmith and Sheridan.*

This volume contains Wilde's four great comedies, all of which bear a quality as personal and as striking as any in English literature. At a time when Victorian platitudes, long the axioms of life on the stage, had begun to lose their force, Wilde seemed to be turning them upside-down or wrong side out, showing that they worked nearly as well either way. Wilde's elegant dialogue, sparkling proverbs and mordant mots are as apt today as when they were first heard. They will delight readers for many years to come.

UL-56

PRIDE AND PREJUDICE

By Jane Austen

Jane Austen's *brilliant comedy of manners has amused and delighted readers for more than a century. Its enduring qualities are those inherent in Miss Austen's great artistry as a novelist — in her superb ability to create living characters and in her skill as a social satirist of the most delicate kind.*

She treated the society in which she lived with a lightly ironic touch. She was concerned with the complex details of respectable life, the little perplexities of emotion and conduct which were the never-ending problems of her country gentlefolk. Miss Austen was of that society herself, yet she had the rare ability to see things as they were, objectively but sympathetically.

Pride and Prejudice *is basically a love story — the chronicle of a long courtship in which the hero's pride and the heroine's prejudice are the primary obstacles to a well-suited marriage. It is Miss Austen's sense of dramatic progression that makes this romance into one of the most fascinating in all literature.*

UL-58

NINE PLAYS OF CHEKOV

THE *delicate capture of a passing mood, the keen sympathy with the Hamlet in all human beings, the poignant probing of an overwhelming frustration—these are the elements which make up Chekov's dramatic vision of life. These plays of the twilight make Chekov, to the Russia of today, perhaps more alien than any other writer of the first rank, though he has been a major influence upon dramatists of the West.*

Perhaps Chekov's basic contribution to the stage can be summed up in the statement that he de-theatricalized the theatre. His plays end, as T. S. Eliot might say, not with a bang but a whimper. He demonstrates that tragedy can be as real in the slow wasting away of lives as in the great dramas of fore-destined catastrophe. He deals with human fate in a minor key.

That Chekov's dramas are of enduring appeal is proven by repeated revivals of his works. This volume, containing four of his major plays and five one-act masterpieces, also provides a valuable chronological table of the playwright's life and works. UL-59

McSORLEY'S WONDERFUL SALOON

By Joseph Mitchell

Most of the twenty stories in this book are about low-life in New York City. Mr. Mitchell presents an admiring description of the eccentricities of the owners and customers of McSorley's, the oldest and most independent saloon in the city, whose bartenders use four soup bowls instead of a cash register, and whose motto is *"Good Ale, Raw Onions, and No Ladies."*

A few of the citizens who figure in these stories are: MAZIE, the blonde and slangy proprietor of a dime movie house, who roams the Bowery after midnight and is undoubtedly the greatest authority in the world on the habits of male and female bums; PROFESSOR SEA GULL, also known as Joe Gould, who filled 270 composition books with bawdy conversations overheard in Greenwich Village; COMMODORE DUTCH, a sporting man, who makes a living by giving an annual ball for the benefit of himself; LADY OLGA, the greatest bearded lady in the history of the American sideshow; and PAPA HOUDINI, a Harlem Calypso singer, among whose songs are *"Old Man You Too Old, You Too Bold, In Fact You Too Cold"* and *"I Like Bananas Because They Have No Bones."* **UL-60**

CRIME AND PUNISHMENT
By
FYODOR DOSTOEVSKY

IT WOULD *probably be appalling to count the number of intelligent readers who have been put off from reading* Crime and Punishment *by its curious reputation as a classic of gloom — both classic and gloominess somehow suggest dullness. Nothing could be farther from Dostoevsky's masterpiece than the suggestion of dullness — disturbing, yes, even terrifying, but* Crime and Punishment *is more thrilling than any novel ever written to provide thrills.*

As Dorothy Brewster says in the introduction to this edition: "The plot, simple enough in outline, is full of breathless suspense and hair-raising episodes. It may be taken quite naively as one of the most thrilling of detective stories. Or just as naively — but more solemnly — as a Christian drama of sin and retribution...or into it may be read psychological, philosophical, and even metaphysical significance, to the limit of one's capacity for such speculation. On whatever levels of response it touches the reader's imagination, it is certain to be a disturbing experience." UL-63

NIJINSKY

By

ROMOLA NIJINSKY

THERE *are many who believe Nijinsky to have been the greatest male dancer of all time. The life of this "God of the Dance" was no less extraordinary than his talents. As an artist of genius he was driven to find an almost solitary perfection with which there could be no compromise. As a human being, he traveled in the darkest realms of inner conflict until he reached the most irrevocable human prison of all — insanity. This is the brilliantly dramatic story of his tumultuous and amazing life, written by the person who knew him best — his wife.*

Here is what some of the critics have written about this great and unusual biography:

"Mme. Nijinsky's book is impressive from a number of angles. It is a biography of extreme personal intensity, devoted, anguished, and, in the best sense, controversial. It embodies information not to be had in any other form concerning one of the first and most unappreciated of all arts — dancing."

LINCOLN KIRSTEIN

"The book is a brilliant storehouse of the ideas that led the Russian ballet forward from their first beginnings to an invasion of Europe. The analyses of the various dances, for which the author has often the authority of Nijinsky himself, are invaluable. The account is in the end humbling and beautiful: it is not often that a writer has seen close at hand the working of a great genius."

UL-62   STARK YOUNG

MISTER JELLY ROLL

By

ALAN LOMAX

SINCE *its first appearance in 1950, this biography of Ferdinand "Jelly Roll" Morton by Alan Lomax has become a classic of jazz literature. Not only is it the biography of one of the great jazz musicians of all time, it is also the story of a new kind of music that rose out of America's Southland to become the music of the twentieth century.*

The Chicago Tribune *wrote: "Alan Lomax has fashioned a biography that, for utter candor and spontaneity of utterance, rivals the self-revelations of Rousseau and St. Augustine."*

And the San Francisco Chronicle *wrote: "You begin to get a fresh idea of what was behind the development of the new music that said so many things to so many people. You see that jazz was actually a 'cultural transmutation,' as Mr. Lomax puts it, 'a wordless counterpoint of protest and of pride.' No one with even the slightest feeling for the subject can afford to miss this book."*

UL-64

MADAME BOVARY

By

GUSTAVE FLAUBERT

MADAME BOVARY *has been called the first modern novel. Its influence on subsequent writers has been profound enough to warrant that description. Flaubert's magnificent achievement was to present a perfect perception of his characters with perfect objectivity. The result in* MADAME BOVARY *was a new kind of realism that shocked its first readers to the core. It remains for readers today just as impressive an experience. The tragedy of Emma Bovary is inexorable and belongs to the grand tradition of tragedy, but it is peculiarly modern, too. There is no appeal to the gods or to fate, no suggestion of a deus ex machina, however disguised. Step by step, with every action and motivation almost frighteningly real, Emma makes her own tragedy—and every other character is equally fully conceived. It is as if Flaubert had created whole people rather than characters of fiction and had then abandoned them to work out their own lives. But a closer examination reveals that this impression is achieved only through the most exquisitely painstaking craft.*

UL-57